A Beginner's Guide to
Living on the
Waterways

A BEGINNER'S GUIDE TO
LIVING ON THE
WATERWAYS

NICK CORBLE AND ALLAN FORD

The
History
Press

First published 2017

The History Press
The Mill, Brimscombe Port
Stroud, Gloucestershire, GL5 2QG
www.thehistorypress.co.uk

British Library Cataloguing in Publication Data.
A catalogue record for this book is available from the British Library.

ISBN 978 0 7509 6990 1

Typesetting and origination by The History Press
Printed and bound in India by Replika Press Pvt. Ltd.

CONTENTS

THE AUTHORS

There is not much Allan Ford doesn't know about narrowboats. Not only does he live on one himself, but he has also spent many years servicing and fixing them. His experience ranges from the mechanical through to the minutiae of day-to-day living, and he brings this to life in these pages, offering hints and tips and helping the potential liveaboard to avoid some of the more obvious, and some of the less obvious, pitfalls of life afloat, as well as ideas on how to get the most out of this uniquely attractive way of life. This is Allan's fifth book; his others (also written with Nick Corble) chronicle the history of his other great passion, fairgrounds, specifically the fairground attraction The Wall of Death. His email is indianscoutrider@hotmail.com.

Nick Corble has written extensively on the canals, both in book form and articles for waterways magazines and the national press. His first book *Walking on Water* described in honest detail his own initiation into the world of the inland waterways, as he bought his first narrowboat and negotiated the spine of the inland waterways system on the eve of the millennium. He followed this up with *James Brindley: The First Canal Builder*, in which he described how, through a combination of personal vision and determination, the canal system first came about. Subsequent works have sought to provide practical advice and guidance to those keen to share his appreciation of the canals. Further details on Nick's writing, which includes both fiction and non-fiction, can be found on his website www.nickcorble.co.uk, where he can also be contacted.

INTRODUCTION

There is something terribly romantic about living on board a boat. Who hasn't, at some point, yearned for that sense of independence, of being the master of one's own destiny? The thought of living on a boat offers both symbolic and tangible advantages. Surrounded by water, with the ability to cast off whenever you feel like it, and in so doing letting go of the burdens and responsibilities of modern life, can seem an alluring prospect. Little wonder, therefore, that every year a growing number do just that, joining the thousands who have already found a way of making the dream come alive. This book is aimed at those tempted to join them, and for those that do, to help make sure that their personal dream doesn't become a nightmare.

Buying a boat and living on it is a relatively simple task, but understanding and coping with the practicalities of living aboard is something that tends to come with time. By condensing decades of experience of living aboard and setting it out into easy-to-follow chapters, our objective in this book is to provide some short cuts and pointers, both for would-be 'liveaboards' and for those who have already made the leap – after all, you're never too old to learn! Not everything can be taught, however, and everyone who makes that leap onto the water will find their own compromises and rhythm needed to make a success of their new life, even if lessons sometimes have to be learned the hard way!

There is no single template for a successful liveaboard life. It is estimated that over 15,000 people live aboard a boat in the UK and like their boats these people are all different. Some choose to live afloat by preference, others for convenience, some because they see it as a way of getting on the property ladder; whilst still more may have little choice but to do so. Some stay there permanently, and others for part of the year only. Some never stray from their moorings, while for others constant movement is the very point of being on a boat. Whilst these considerations may colour different individuals' priorities, there are some challenges that face them all, and this book is all about understanding and meeting these challenges. The emphasis throughout is a combination of hard-nosed practical advice and questions each individual needs to consider, with each chapter ending with a checklist of things to ponder. Where issues are more complex or technical, we have also provided pointers towards sources of further information.

The History Press first asked us to produce a guide to living on a boat nearly ten years ago, and the result of this was our book *Living Aboard*, which we have used as the basis of this book. We have updated where required and tweaked the emphasis, where appropriate, in the light of changing circumstances, including a change of title to better reflect the book's aspirations. We have also taken the opportunity to refresh most of the illustrations that accompany the text. Many of the basics of liveaboard life remain the same, but other facets of life on the waterways have changed since the first version of this book. Most fundamentally, the body overseeing much of our inland network has changed from British Waterways to the Canal and River Trust, a move that has seen a shift in approach that some have welcomed, others perhaps less so. Technical regulations and requirements have also been revised in some areas, and these are open to regular review. As such, whilst the advice given here was correct at the time of writing, the prudent would-be boater should check for further changes post-publication.

When we were writing *Living Aboard* the waterways faced an existential threat, a danger that has now thankfully passed. Indeed, in the period since then the media seem to have been conducting a love affair with the waterways, with a number of celebrities 'discovering', or suddenly needing to share their love of the canal network. The programmes and articles that have flowed since have only served to highlight the many aesthetic attractions of the waterways. At the same time, the 'credit crunch' and its aftermath has brought to the fore the very real practical advantages living on the waterways can offer for many, especially in our cities. It is a little-known fact, for example, that more people live on boats in London (and Oxford, Birmingham and Manchester) than do so in Venice.

Those contemplating a life afloat will need to balance these 'heart' and 'head' considerations, and it is our hope that this book will help in that process. The information we provide is based largely upon experience and is necessarily subjective. Others may not share our views, and we would recommend that anyone keen to make the next step talks to as many knowledgeable people as possible, from towpath chats to detailed discussions with professionals.

Living aboard offers a host of pleasures, but it isn't for everyone. If it turns out to be for you, we hope that this book makes some small contribution to making your life better once you finally get afloat. If, having read this book, you decide that maybe it's not for you after all, then hopefully we have helped also.

Finally, we would like to thank the following for their time and assistance in compiling this book, and in particular allowing us to photograph them at work: Tooley's Boatyard in Banbury, Oxfordshire Narrowboats, Heyford Marina, Kingsground Narrowboats, Safeshore Marine, Jez Boat Painting Services, Mike Walker Boat Services, The Wharf at Bridge 190 and Midland Chandlers in Braunston. All the photos in the book are by the authors except where otherwise indicated.

CHAPTER I

THE FLOATING CITIZEN

L iving aboard a boat is something many people may contemplate at some point in their lives, although only relatively few ever actually make the leap. There are a number of reasons for this, both practical and psychological. The purpose of this book is to explore these reasons in greater depth, both to help those thinking about a floating home make an informed choice, and to provide valuable insight on key practicalities for those who do decide to go ahead.

Given this practical focus, as the reader progresses through the chapters the list of potential obstacles and bases to cover may begin to snowball to a point where they conclude that only the most foolhardy would ever contemplate a life aboard. That is not the intention. Rather, the aim is to guide you through the issues a potential liveaboard needs to consider and to break them down so they become manageable rather than potentially overwhelming.

Having said that, if the negatives accumulate to a point where the balance of consideration leans rather too heavily into the debit column, then it's likely that you lack the mix of temperament, skills, finances, or simply appetite, to make a success of life afloat – and as such it's likely these pages will have saved you a lot of anguish and cash. If, on the other hand, you remain undaunted by the challenges covered here, and maybe even feel energised by them – and we hope you are – then the book will also have done its job, helping to equip you for a successful future afloat, and hopefully allowing you to bypass some of the more obvious mistakes.

In considering a life afloat, it is the practical challenges which are in many ways easier to cope with, since very few of the problems that you might encounter will not have cropped up before, and if you are reading this, it may well be precisely because you are keen to learn from the experience of those who have 'been there, done that'. The psychological side of things is harder to pin down, and whilst the rest of this book tends to focus on the practical, the opening two chapters are more about the fundamental, less tangible, considerations to be taken into account before joining the liveaboard community.

Some moorings can get a bit crowded.

Is some kind of floating house your dream?

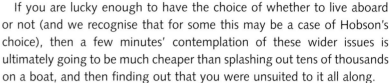

If you are lucky enough to have the choice of whether to live aboard or not (and we recognise that for some this may be a case of Hobson's choice), then a few minutes' contemplation of these wider issues is ultimately going to be much cheaper than splashing out tens of thousands on a boat, and then finding out that you were unsuited to it all along.

The good news is that wanting to live afloat is not the first sign of madness. To put things in perspective, a population at least equivalent to that of Reigate – that's nearly twice the size of the average UK town – lives on boats in the UK. Unlike the inhabitants of Reigate, however, it is easy for this population to become forgotten citizens. Unlike the house-dweller, they cannot take for granted those facets of modern life that we have come to assume as the basics of a civilised society, such as on-demand electricity, gas, water, sewage, telephone and internet access. Whether moored or moving, the boat-dweller – metaphorically and sometimes literally – takes the conscious decision to take on responsibility for accessing these amenities, rather than assuming someone else will provide them automatically, and perhaps less consciously, from much else that society offers.

What previously simply arrived or was taken for granted becomes something that has to be actively procured. If your water or electricity suddenly runs out, then you will probably only have yourself to blame rather than some abstract provider. The good news is, securing these services is relatively straightforward and options for doing so are covered in subsequent chapters. Other 'rights' that we may take for granted are more difficult to pin down, and may only become obvious on an occasional basis, or in times of crisis, but are just as important as components of a civilised lifestyle, and some of these are explored later in this chapter.

It is worth recognising that one person's perceived 'right' might be another's choice. For some, part of the attraction of a life afloat may be to deliberately disavow what might be considered 'traditional' ways of living; after all, what's the point of living on a boat if all you do is create a floating house? This ambition to live 'off the grid' or 'off the land' presents fresh challenges. These are covered in greater depth in the following chapter but are raised here to recognise, and perhaps illustrate the point, that there are probably as many motivations for the liveaboard life as there are liveaboards.

Articulating what that motivation might be may not be as straight-forward as it sounds. Is it driven by the wish to relinquish or move away from restraints you feel are currently holding you back from living how you want to live, or is it the result of certain definable attractions that will provide the missing piece of the jigsaw? In other words, are you trying to move away from a certain way of living or move towards one? Are you chasing a romantic dream that needs to be tested, or is it something you always thought you'd do when you retired and are ploughing on with without really testing why?

A useful first step therefore can be to attempt some form of clarification of your motivations, perhaps through a self-assessment, or perhaps by getting someone to conduct a friendly cross-examination with you. Ask yourself basic questions such as what you are looking forward to the most and what you might miss the most. In doing so, it can also be useful to consider what features of your future life you might be prepared to be flexible on, and which you might regard as non-negotiable.

Equipped with this understanding, a good place to continue is to think about what sort of person you are, and the type of environment you tend to be comfortable in. Whether you are the social type or a bit of a loner (and the liveaboard community tends to weigh disproportionately towards the extremes of the spectrum) is likely to have a huge bearing on your lifestyle afloat. Are you the sort of person who needs daily contact with others, or are you quite happy with your own company?

Are you the type of person who prefers solitude?

If it's possible to find out beforehand, understanding the type of people who tend to congregate around, and the general 'vibe' of, particular kinds of moorings, may be critical in choosing where you want to be. Designated towpath runs of liveaboard moorings, for example, may have more of a community feel, whilst a mooring out on its own is, by definition, more isolated. Some marinas, especially those with a clubhouse, may be sociable, whilst others may be full of occasional boaters and have no life to them at all. This assumes, of course, that you want to have a base, even if you do not spend all of your time there. As later chapters will show, this may not necessarily be the case.

If a more isolated setting is your preference, then it is worth contemplating the different degrees of isolation available. The legacy of our inland waterways system means that there is no shortage of options when choosing where you might live afloat, be it a marina, canal, river or coastal estuary, but ours is also a compact island and most of these are close to some kind of civilisation and you'd have to be fairly determined to cut yourself off completely.

Taking the issue of sociability to the next level is the question of whether you want to live alone or share your boat with others. Again, this is not always a matter of choice, but it is a matter worth consideration.

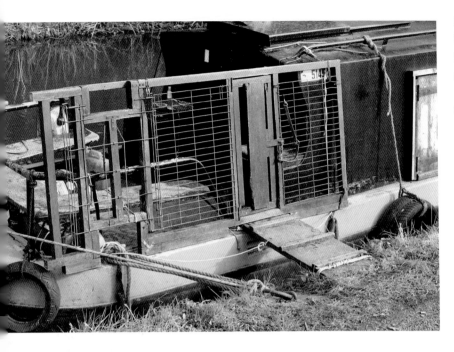

Having a dog may mean having to take precautions to keep them from running off.

Boats are, by definition, confined spaces and, depending on who's on board, this will have different implications. If you are on your own – and this tends to be the majority amongst liveaboards – is this something you are comfortable with, or is there even a slight potential for 'cabin fever'? If you are with someone else, how much do you all need 'your own space' every now and then?

A favoured option for company amongst many liveaboards is to have a pet, with dogs a popular choice, not least because they tend to be more comfortable around water than cats, although caged pets such as rabbits are not unknown. Dogs also tend to be easier to retrieve than cats when it's time to leave a mooring and can also act as a good deterrent to unwelcome visitors. They will need exercise – by definition there is little to be had inside a boat – and considerations about getting them on and off the boat in awkward moorings may also come into play, as well as what might be the most appropriate breed. If you are not a 'doggy person', the preferences of those around you may be a further thing to take into account when selecting a mooring, especially if it is a permanent one: others might be!

It is also worth considering whether you regard life afloat as a permanent or a temporary state. If it's the latter, you may wish to at least think about how you are eventually going to return to dry land. For example, some live aboard to coincide with a particular time in their lives – a short-term job, for example, or perhaps while they are studying. Others may do so through a lack of alternatives, driven by an event such as a divorce or a shortage of funds, and then find themselves trapped with no way of returning to a 'normal' way of life in a house, although as we will see, 'normal' has a way of redefining itself when you choose a boat as your home. Still others may be 'seasonal' boaters, living on board a boat from spring to autumn, but having a base to see them through the winter.

Living aboard offers real benefits that compensate for the inevitable compromises that will have to be made. The trick is not to see these as second best, just different. Making the psychological adjustment to being a permanent liveaboard is something that takes at least a year, and probably a minimum of two winters. It involves acquiring a new set of habits and expectations from life, while gradually a fresh perspective dawns, creeping up on you so that others begin to notice the changes in you more than you do yourself. You value things differently, you appreciate aspects of your environment you either took for granted or hardly noticed before, and, like someone deprived of their sight, gain a heightened sensitivity to other aspects of your personality. It's not an instant conversion though, and too many potential liveaboards give up before their epiphany. So when things aren't going so well, remember that this is a long-term commitment and, like a new marriage, is something that has to be worked at.

Assuming you're still game, the remainder of this chapter considers those issues that lie somewhere between the purely psychological and clearly practical. These include matters which are generally considered rights in a civilised society, but which may have to be worked at to be secured. What is more, the ways of achieving them may vary from area to area, leading to a lack of certainty that may, according to your predisposition, be either extremely frustrating or all part of the fun!

Let's start with the most basic consideration of all when it comes to avoiding becoming some kind of anonymous 'non-person' as far as bureaucracy is concerned. You will have a National Insurance number and NHS number (it's worth knowing what this is, and it's not always easy to find), and probably a bank account, but what you won't have if you are on the move is a postcode. It's worth having one of these, even if it's nominal, for reasons that will become obvious. Grown-up children, other relatives, or very good friends, can be handy in this regard. Before starting life as a liveaboard, it may be handy to renew things like your passport and driving licence using your nominal postcode, as these can then act as a 'proof of address' or identity for those that need them.

If we have officialdom out of the picture, the most fundamental issue is probably your health, and maintaining it. Living a more active life, with a fair sprinkling of physical labour, it seems reasonable to assume you will be less susceptible to health problems. However, that very activity also opens you up to the odd mishap, and of course there are the unpredictable niggles to cope with. What happens when things go wrong, especially if you are on your own? What if you are far from the nearest road and an ambulance, paramedic, doctor, nurse or even a vet for your dog can't get to you?

The misery of even niggling complaints can multiply when you've only your cabin and a bunk to see them off in, and even more so when keeping warm means getting out of your bed to stoke the fire, or worse, having to go outside to fetch some coal or change a gas bottle. The potential hazards of 'cabin fever' have also already been mentioned, and the danger of mental illness should not be dismissed, especially for those whose motivations for living aboard were complicated in the first place.

On the practical side, there's also the consideration of where you stand with regard to accessing health services, something we would never question if we lived on dry land. The NHS is not necessarily geared up for those of 'no fixed abode' and if you are not careful there is a danger that you can involuntarily elect to become a 'non-person' by choosing a life afloat. This is one area where a postcode can come in handy. Of course, hospitals will admit you if something disastrous occurs, but what if your needs are more ongoing – the management of a chronic complaint, for example – or if you need an entry point into the health system?

Traditionally, the latter has been provided by GPs, but the services provided through GP practices, and the range of healthcare professionals within them, have become more diverse and harder to pin down in recent years. GPs are not obliged to accept you onto their rolls, and even if they were willing, registration may not be practical if you intend to be on the move for significant lengths of time. This can be a serious consideration for the permanent on-the-move boater, although seasonal liveaboards will probably find it easier to register from their winter base and, if necessary, register as a guest at a practice if the need arises when they are away from that base.

Should the latter become necessary, you are likely to be asked how long you are staying, as the GP will only want to supply you with enough medication to last until you are off their patch, something to bear in mind should you be at the point of leaving. Otherwise, if you have a repeat prescription, you will probably need to organise this from your 'main' GP if you are a seasonal liveaboard, and make arrangements for someone to pick up the prescription and mail it on to an address where you know you are going to be.

If GP practices have become more complex in recent years, so have hospital-based services. It is dangerous to assume every hospital will have an A&E – with drop-in centres, out of hours centres, specific clinics and triage centres all possibilities. The internet can help in determining where you can go (assuming you have access to it), and equally the NHS 111 non-emergency number can help, again, assuming you have a telephone signal.

Similar thought also needs to be given to access to other parts of the welfare state such as pensions, post offices and social services, other areas where a postcode will help fend off questions; and special consideration is needed if you intend to live aboard with small children or with pets. If you think it may be difficult getting access to a GP, this is nothing compared to gaining access to a dentist or a vet, especially if it is an emergency.

All this is not to underestimate the value of support mechanisms within the boating community. Depending on your circumstances, but following

Some system for picking up your post is
likely to be required.

the 'there but for the grace of God' principle, fellow-boaters tend to be more than willing to help out a neighbour in distress. If you are known on a mooring it's unlikely that you will have to worry about someone looking after your boat if you are called away, but if you aren't, this may be a consideration.

Continuing the floating citizen theme is the issue of making your voice heard. Every citizen has a right to vote unless they are a peer or are in prison. But if you are a liveaboard – the ultimate 'floating voter' – it may seem at times as if a third category has been added. To vote you must be registered in a particular area, which may be tricky if the area you are living in changes most days. Postal voting is one option, but has to be organised.

Equally, being a citizen carries responsibilities and one of these is to pay taxes. The authorities may be slow to grant you your vote, but you can be pretty certain that they'll be a lot quicker in claiming your contribution. One particular area of potential complication is council tax. The rules of this tax are open to a host of different interpretations by local authorities, and if you are thinking about a permanent mooring, it is worth checking out the local situation, which can vary greatly. The Residential Boat Owners' Association (www.rboa.org.uk) is a useful source on information on this subject.

Another intangible is communications. Being on the move or down a gated towpath may make it difficult for the postman to reach you, and even though traditional 'snail mail' post isn't as important as it used to be, a mechanism for collecting letters and parcels is necessary. Options may include a 'care of' host address, for example at a marina, or a PO Box, and parcels can increasingly be directed towards collection points at retail premises. Alternatively, services such as www.boatmail.co.uk offer a comprehensive mail forwarding system as well as a free UK street address, all for a low 'pay as you go' fee.

As already suggested, some boaters find it useful to have an 'accommodation address', provided by a willing friend or relative, to act as a means of interacting with bureaucracy, an approach that has the benefit of providing someone capable of opening a communication, or at least deciding whether it is important, rather than having it rest in a PO Box. This approach may be less suitable for anyone claiming benefits.

Whichever route you take on this issue, bear in mind that the daily rattle of the letterbox may become a thing of the past if you live aboard. Less reliance on post presupposes access to electronic communications, a topic covered in more detail later in this book, but before leaving the issue of communications it's worth noting that most boats are made of steel, and steel and mobile signals do not go together well. Anyone fancy taking that important call from the bank standing outside in the rain balanced on the gunwale?

A side effect of not having a regular address is the difficulty that this can cause with banking. Banks seem to be obsessed with customers having a fixed abode and the utility bills to prove it. As a result, assuming you don't go for the 'holding address' option, it can be a good idea to create your own version of 'offshore' banking before you make the leap away from bricks and mortar. Electronic banking is fairly standard these days, but be aware of security, notably the Wi-Fi systems you might be using, and it's best to avoid banking using internet cafés or other public systems. Boaters tend to value cash more, but this raises its own issues of security both on board and when out and about, although generic ATMs are fairly widespread.

As highlighted already, all this assumes that putative liveaboards are trying to replicate life on dry land. It's just as possible that part of the attraction is that they relish the thought of no more junk mail, spam email, Facebook friend requests, nuisance phone calls and CCTV (although most marinas operate CCTV systems). As with most things, the secret lies in achieving a happy balance but at the risk of being repetitive and as subsequent chapters will demonstrate, this is something that has to be worked at. Living aboard involves a new set of rules, rules that you need to flex into, not fight. You need to start out from the viewpoint that compromises will have to be made. The question is, which are the things you are prepared to sacrifice the most easily and which are you prepared to go the extra mile to achieve?

Someone once made the analogy between someone who becomes a liveaboard but constantly complains that things aren't what they're used to with someone who decides to become a vegetarian but keeps buying mock-meat products. The secret to being comfortable with the liveaboard lifestyle lies with the three 'A's: *accept* its rules, *adopt* its mentality and *adapt* it to suit your own particular needs and desires. If this is something you think you can do, the rest of this book will, we hope, prove to be invaluable.

Living aboard can get complicated!

Would you miss not having a garden?

> **?** What is your motivation for wanting to be a liveaboard – is it a necessity or a choice? How much room for manoeuvring do you have? Have you or your partner ever had a holiday afloat?

> **?** Do you enjoy practical challenges?

> **?** Are you used to 'roughing it' occasionally – have you enjoyed camping or caravan holidays in the past?

> **?** How much do you need daily contact with other people?

> **?** How much do you and possible companions value your 'personal space'?

> **?** Are you likely to need good access to health and social support?

> **?** How comfortable are you about a partial 'opting out' from mainstream society?

> **?** How much do you need 'instant' access to the wider world?

CHAPTER 2

ALTERNATIVE LIFESTYLES

For many, the decision to embrace the liveaboard life may be an entirely pragmatic one, driven as much as anything by finance and circumstance. For others, the attraction is less tangible, with living on board a boat, almost by definition, offering an alternative lifestyle to what others might regard as conventional. However, what different individuals mean by 'alternative' will vary. It may for example encompass a desire to get more in touch with nature and reduce one's carbon footprint, whilst at the far end of the spectrum it may be more radical than this, a rejection of all the hassles and pressures of modern life and everything that comes with it.

The latter is sometimes described as going 'off-grid', an aspiration that encompasses, in strict terms, a wish to disconnect with formal utility grids such as water, electricity and gas, but has come to mean something broader: a withdrawal from the need for these and other services such as banking, telephony, shops and so on altogether, to become invisible to conventional society and reliant only on yourself.

For others, the drive behind becoming a liveaboard may be more to do with freedom, a sense of not being tied down and going where your heart is pulling you, of revelling in the ability to loosen the ropes and, quite literally, cast off into the unknown whenever you feel like it. Equally, freedom may take other forms, to do less with movement and more with detachment, being part of an urban or rural community just not surrounded by bricks and mortar.

Motivations for becoming a liveaboard will cover a broad spectrum of impulses, all of them highly individual and many of them overlapping, with some of them more realistic than others. Becoming a liveaboard is seen by some as a permanent shift, whilst others may see it as a temporary arrangement, designed to get them over a particular hump in their lives. One person's 'alternative' may be another's 'mainstream', and as such a more accurate title for this chapter may have required a question mark after it.

Considering and understanding your motivation for becoming a liveaboard before you set out can help provide some useful parameters

Liveaboards and the authorities do
not always see eye to eye.

Using the roof to store wood and
keep plants.

for key decisions down the line. The purpose of this chapter therefore is to offer some hints and tips, and possibly also some reality checks, on different versions of alternative lifestyles to help inform the development of that understanding.

A Greener Alternative

Although it may not seem like it when your engine blows out a cloud of black smoke on starting up, the simple fact of living on a boat is likely to result in a reduced carbon footprint. The environmental impact of fabricating a boat is a fraction of that of building a house, and many last just as long. They also require much less energy to maintain both the fabric and the occupants inside on an ongoing basis.

Beyond this basic fact, living on a boat also offers a number of possibilities for a greener lifestyle and reducing that footprint even further. One of the most fundamental aspects of boat living is the opportunity it provides to become more attuned with the seasons, not least because your heating is likely to be something you regulate for yourself rather than relying on a thermostat to do the job for you. With this comes an almost primeval desire to start growing things. Rare is the liveaboard boat that doesn't carry at least some pots or grow bags with budding produce or, where circumstances permit, a small plot on the towpath or nearby. Tomatoes, peppers, herbs, courgettes and salad leaves all lend themselves to small-scale growing, whilst a stretch of land may also open up the possibility of beans, brassicas and even potatoes. The trick, as with so many things on board, is to be selective and to use your limited space well.

Growing isn't the only option, with the foraging of wild fruit and other produce also a possibility. Autumnal hedgerow fruits such as blackberries, elderberries and sloes are an obvious target here, although other less often considered options include stinging nettles, funghi (check first!) and wild watercress, which should only be picked from fast-flowing streams as they can include parasites. Further underrated wild foods include nuts, which are full of protein – especially chestnuts and hazelnuts, with the latter tasting a bit like peas.

Boaters have an additional advantage when it comes to foraging, namely ready access to the water, with the top of the list in terms of abundance probably the unloved American signal crayfish, an import that has practically seen off the indigenous variety. Prolific and aggressive, these are easy to catch by lowering a net with some kind of bait and waiting.

Hedgerow fruits are a good source of free food in the autumn.

Crayfish straight from the canal.

Catching freshwater mussels.

Recycling becomes a habit for the liveaboard.

Freshwater mussels can also be caught simply by tickling them with a reed;the mussels will clamp the reed, allowing them to be lifted out of the water. Pigeons and rabbits are also an option for those who know how to catch them, and can be cooked over an open fire, saving fuel.

Foraging isn't just about food, with wood usually in abundant supply in the countryside, and spotting wood supplies on a boat is often a clear sign that the occupant is a seasoned liveaboard. Those with the time and inclination can also gather wool from barbed wire fences, which can be washed, spun and knitted, although a simpler option may be to buy a second-hand jumper from a charity shop for a couple of pounds!

The growing season is a short one in the UK, so the canny boater also tends to become adept at old skills of preserving and pickling, especially as freezers are rarely a realistic option on a boat. Jars of fruit or chutney can then be traded on the towpath for variety. The fuel involved in making chutney may outweigh the benefits, although a stove can often be pressed into action for simmering, and the same may be true for baking bread.

Adopting a greener lifestyle is about being resourceful and keeping your eyes and ears open to opportunities. Old tyres can be used as planters or fenders, for example, and decent bicycles can be picked up for next to nothing from most recycling centres or from police auctions, and websites such as www.freecycle.org and www.gumtree.com, as well as local free ads in good old-fashioned newspapers can often be excellent sources for free stuff. When space is at a premium and you have a greater awareness of where things come from (and where they go when you've finished with them), a greener lifestyle tends to become a state of mind rather than an effort. A good example of this is recycling, which in the absence of regular kerbside rubbish collections tends to become a necessity rather than a chore, especially as liveaboards tend to use more tins and glass than most households. Decent access to boaters' disposal and recycling points becomes a significant consideration.

Disappearing

Who hasn't at some point felt like stopping the world and just getting off? Some of those attracted to becoming a liveaboard see a life afloat as an opportunity to do just that, a chance to slip away and disappear on your own personal lifeboat, staying one step ahead of the powers-that-be. The first thing to say is that creating your own personal lifeboat is relatively straightforward. Going truly 'off-grid' on the other hand is much, much harder. The reality is that slipping completely off the radar of bureaucracy requires sacrificing many of the benefits associated with being part of a civilised society described in the previous chapter, and even if one was prepared to make this sacrifice, the powers you are trying to escape from are unlikely to give up keeping you on their screens without a fight.

The rise of the 'surveillance society', both overtly through measures such as CCTV, and less obviously through the tracing of mobile phones or financial transactions, has made it much harder to disappear than perhaps it once might have been. This is not to say that some semblance of disconnecting with the modern world is impossible, just that it requires determination, and anyone thinking they can simply disappear and live in perfect isolation on a boat is probably living in a fool's paradise.

As a minimum, while your boat may be wandering free, every vessel on the waterways system has to be anchored, albeit virtually, to an address. Those responsible for running the waterways have in recent years become assiduous in policing the licensing of boats, which in turn requires having an address somewhere. These requirements are covered in more detail later on in this book, but they are hard facts that cannot be ignored. As such, just having a boat on the waterways system will require a compromise with the wider 'system', assuming of course you wish to stay within the law.

Beyond this basic fact, there are other considerations, where there is perhaps greater room for negotiation. Food, water, fuel and money are rudimentaries for anyone, but acquiring them can be achieved in a number of ways. This chapter has already explored some of the options on growing or foraging for food and fuel for keeping warm, and water is generally not a problem assuming you have paid your boat licence and can legitimately use the water points provided on the system – although it is worth pointing out that some water points on rivers can charge. Later chapters in this book will also consider accessing power from renewable sources.

It is difficult (although not totally impossible) to live without money, and the balance between the need for it, or to access accumulated funds, and the extent to which fresh supplies of it need to be generated, will also be a key determinant in how 'off-grid' an individual can go. Furthermore, liveaboards are entitled to (and many rely on) benefits, and accessing them will inevitably require some level of contact with the authorities. Bartering goods and services can help, but certain basics such as the boat licence (again!) and diesel and coal (if required) will almost certainly need hard cash, although this may be possible through a proxy, allowing an individual to remain clear of 'the system'. On the subject of diesel, options exist around biofuels made from recycled cooking oils, and it may be easier to trade with the makers of this than your local fuel supplier.

Biodiesel recycled from cooking oil can be used on boats.

Perhaps the biggest consideration when deciding whether to go 'off-grid' is the by-product of the act of doing so, namely isolation. Cutting yourself off from society also removes you from the comforts and protection it affords. 'Off-gridders' tend to be solo travellers (doing so as a couple roughly doubles your chance of being 'found'), and may indeed self-define themselves as the types who can not only survive but thrive on their own, but it is worth checking in on this before taking what might be a momentous step. As later chapters in this book will demonstrate, creating an acceptable equilibrium between 'needs' and 'wants' is often a case of recognising individual comfort zones, and that is as true in the need for interaction with wider society as it is with anything.

Town and Country

One of the most significant trends in boat living in recent years has been the significant growth in urban liveaboards. Often this has been driven by necessity, particularly in London, where housing costs have escalated to the point where only the very rich can dream of owning, or often even renting, a place to live. As such, it should come as no surprise that growing numbers of people have spotted the pragmatic solution that living on board offers, and equally that this can lead to tensions between those charged with running the waterways, who have their own agenda, and those who want to live on them, who have theirs.

If you can make it work, urban boat living has much to recommend it, especially if you need to work in the same environment or want to access all that urban life has to offer in terms of entertainment and culture. At the same time, urban moorings can offer particular security challenges if not in a designated secure site such as a marina or boating club, and here lies the rub – the demand for designated residential urban moorings far outstrips supply. Those faced with little alternative other than to live on a boat in order to stay living in the city are increasingly challenging existing guidelines on what may or may not constitute a long-term or residential mooring, and this is happening at a time when those responsible for making those designations in the first place are becoming firmer in their attitude to policing them.

Although this problem is not confined to London, it is particularly acute there, and in April 2016 the Canal and River Trust announced the development of a strategy designed to make a 'significant difference to the capital's canals, listening to the views of 'those who use the capital's canals and rivers', with details of the strategy expected to become available in 2017. What exactly this means is yet to become clear, and it is worth noting that this remit is a wide one, going beyond just those who use the waterways to live on.

Another key point for those considering boat living as a way of solving their urban housing problem is that it is unlikely to prove a permanent solution if it is seen as a way of getting on the housing ladder. Whilst boats, if well maintained and if they have mooring rights in a high-demand area, may appreciate in value, they are unlikely to do so at anything like the rate a bricks and mortar home might. As such, transferring to a home afloat may exacerbate rather than solve a problem, unless it is seen as an expediency to create the space to allow for saving for the deposit for a home, if indeed that is someone's aim. Equally, boat living is unlikely to provide the security of tenure and of rights that more conventional housing tends to offer. As we will see in later chapters, the choice to live on board should been seen as one made for reasons that go beyond the purely financial.

For those for whom it is an option, rural living may offer an alternative. Here the benefits are perhaps equally obvious on first glance: solitude, quiet and closeness to nature to name but three; but considerations of the head need to match those of the heart. Firstly, it should not be assumed that rural boating is necessarily less open to security concerns than its urban equivalent. An isolated boat with easily grabbed belongings can offer a more tempting target than one in a city surrounded by CCTV cameras. Rural moorings may be easier to come by, but they are more likely to need additional support in the form of access to transport (ideally mechanised), which in turn raises the issue of where to keep whatever form of transport opted for.

Rural moorings, certainly those outside of a marina, are also likely to have greater access to towpath or other land, which opens up the possibility of limited cultivation or access to foraging, as discussed above, as well as options for additional storage space, or even just somewhere to hang the washing! That said, there appears to be a decreased tolerance for what is sometimes known as 'towpath colonisation' than in the past, both by the authorities and others who use or live near the waterways, especially as more and more houses are built by canals, with a waterside view now seen to add value.

A final option is not to limit yourself to urban or rural living, but to do both. This is possible through the mechanism of what is known on the waterways as 'continuous cruising' – a category that even has its own form of licence. Conservative estimates suggest those taking this option are a fairly select group of probably around 2,000 boats, although this is not a fixed number, with individuals joining and leaving all the time. Anecdotal evidence suggests, however, that the numbers are rising, and again, as we shall see, this is an area where interpretation of the rules is being tightened up, leading to some friction.

The ins and outs of the regulations surrounding continuous cruising are covered in more detail in Chapter 4, and here we will consider some of the wider considerations this option throws up. Successful continuous cruisers need to be good at planning, by its very nature – and this might appear on the surface to be counter-intuitive – it is not a 'just in time' activity. All possible eventualities have to be planned for, from a sudden loss of power necessitating access to candles, through to making sure you always have your water topped up, your sanitary arrangements emptied out and some spare diesel to hand.

Most importantly, as the name implies, you need to be continuously on the move. The rules dictate you need to move on every fortnight, and that that move needs to be significant (again, this is explained in greater detail in Chapter 4). As soon as you arrive anywhere you need to be thinking about your next move, and like a good chess player you probably need to be thinking three or four moves ahead.

Relative isolation and being cut off from a permanent community can also be an issue for the continuous cruiser, although it is possible to make moving on to a fresh mooring or stocking up on essentials a social affair by involving friends and family – the need to keep on the move is likely to obviate the need to have a car. Equally, continuous cruisers find that boats have an uncanny habit of attracting other boats, and they are rarely alone for long. On the other hand, choosing a new mooring can become something of an art, the continuous cruiser may not want to attract others, and needs to be adept at spotting what makes one mooring safer than others if they are in unfamiliar territory. Neighbours can be good for exchanging information, but they do impose social restraints if you want to maintain good relations, for example on when you can run your engine or create smoke.

Finally on this subject, continuous cruising in winter is complicated by stoppages for maintenance, when whole stretches of canal or individual locks are taken off-limits. The good news is, these can give a cast-iron excuse for not moving (or at least having that discussion with the mooring warden), the bad news is, you may find yourself stuck, and in a worst-case scenario unable to access services. The lesson here is that successful continuous cruisers need to be a balance of adaptable people and good planners.

Urban boat living is becoming an increasingly popular choice.

Looks like washing day!

Questions for Alternative Lifestyles

> ❓ What is your definition of an alternative lifestyle?

> ❓ Is 'going green' a motivator for becoming a liveaboard?

> ❓ Is growing and preserving fruit and vegetables attractive to you?

> ❓ What's your version of 'off-grid'?

> ❓ How comfortable are you with isolation?

> ❓ If contemplating urban living have you checked mooring availability?

> ❓ Make sure you don't see a boat as the first rung of the housing ladder

> ❓ Continuous cruising isn't as easy as it sounds – have you got what it takes?

CHAPTER 3

CHOOSING A BOAT

Having made the decision that you want to live on the water, the next step is to think about what type of boat you want – and then to match that to what you can afford. As anyone operating on a budget knows, 'want' is not necessarily the same as 'need' and potential liveaboards will soon discover that choosing a boat involves a lot of compromise and not a little foresight.

Buying boats is not like buying houses. Any estate agent will tell you that the three most important factors involved with buying a house are location, location and location; but when it comes to liveaboard boats, this is only true if you are planning a permanent mooring, and even that tends to come as a separate entity. When buying a boat there are many different factors involved, but the issue of whether you intend to stay put or whether you intend to cruise – and if you do, how much cruising you intend to do – will probably be one of the most important factors in deciding which type of boat you get.

This question is critical on a number of levels. If you do intend to cruise, then you will need to consider your motive power and the compromises this may force. Most boats require an engine, unless they can be entirely powered by sail or muscle power or are not required to move, although it should be remembered that your engine is also your personal power station. This means an engine room or compartment and somewhere to store fuel, which in turn affects the configuration of your boat, bearing in mind the need to consider the impact of noise, space, vibration and fumes when your boat is also your home.

Just as importantly, your decision on whether or not to cruise will affect the three fundamental questions that the aspiring liveaboard will need to settle. These are explored in greater detail in what follows and are:

❖   What type of waterway do you want to be on?

❖   What type and size of boat will suit you best?

❖   Are you looking for a boat, a house or a houseboat?

Although narrowboats are the favoured craft for liveaboards, they are not the only option.

Although uncommon, canals have been known to flood.

Crowded moorings are becoming a growing problem.

Estuaries are an option – if you don't mind mud!

Types of Waterway

As has already been highlighted, there are plenty of options on places where you can live on a boat on our small island. Four main types of waterway offer a berth: canals, rivers, coasts and estuaries. Each of these offers their own advantages and disadvantages. Being 'dead water' without tides, canals are highly predictable, and although disasters such as breaches or floods aren't unknown they are highly unusual. They are also well geared up for the liveaboard, with plenty of marinas, designated residential moorings and other facilities, and on the canals you are rarely far from the other conveniences of modern living such as banks, supermarkets and launderettes. It is little surprise therefore that canals are the most popular option for liveaboards.

Canal detractors would point out that these features make them all too predictable and even complain of overcrowding in places, a problem that has grown in recent years. The decision of whether or not to cruise also comes in here, as those who do want to wander will find in canals a ready-made network; even if, once again, the canal detractors might be scornful of the pre-packaged nature of the waterways system, with its designated routes and hordes of amateurs and tourists clogging things up for half the year.

Canals also, by their very nature, determine the type of boat you can have. In order to cruise the entire network you will need to have a narrowboat, no more than 6ft 10in wide, although if you are happy to limit yourself to the broad canals you can double this. Most narrowboats are 30ft, 44ft, 50ft, 55ft, 60ft or 70ft long, although the northernmost English canal, the Leeds & Liverpool, has locks that only allow boats of a maximum 60ft in length.

Rivers offer greater scope for boats, but less freedom to cruise. They may also be tidal, which adds another challenge to the choice of moorings and to the range of kit that needs to be carried, such as anchors and lines. Taking the Thames aside, rivers tend to be less busy, but locks can be more of an issue, as can moorings, as they tend to be busier generally. If you have a craft that can cope with coastal waters, however, they can offer a good compromise.

Coastal waters themselves tend to be a whole different ball game. These are obviously tidal and berths for the liveaboard can be hard to come by. Living in coastal waters, the size of your boat is only limited by the size of your wallet, and in contrast to rivers and canals, those living on the coast tend to have more of an external rather than internal perspective. For them a cruise becomes more of a voyage, and one that takes them beyond these shores.

Estuaries tend to be popular for those who want to have something bigger, and in many cases wackier! Although these too are tidal, in practice many liveaboard boats moored on estuaries spend more time on mud than water. Examples of estuary craft can vary from old lighters and barges right through to converted warships and high examples of the do-it-yourself craft, which in many cases fall some way short of ever being seaworthy.

Type and Size of Boat

Your preferred type of waterway will therefore to some extent limit the type and size of boat available. Another key consideration is the number of people who will be living aboard – and don't forget to include any pets – which will determine both the space required and the help available to move your boat around. A particular consideration will be whether you have, or plan to have, small children around, be they your own or grandchildren. But if you are living alone and intend to cruise around you may wish to sacrifice some space in order to have a boat that is easier to handle and look after.

As suggested in the previous chapters, clarity on your motivation and needs will provide an invaluable reference point when it comes to choosing your boat. Whilst many considering a liveaboard life may be basing their decision on experience born of boating holidays, it is important to recognise that what may suffice for a week or two in the summer may prove to be totally inadequate if your boat becomes your home. Equally, whilst it may be tempting to go for the biggest boat you can afford (70ft if you opt for a narrowboat), this may not be so practical if you intend to cruise in it, depending upon your experience and that of your crew. If you decide to go for a longer boat and know you will want to cruise a fair bit, one option at this stage will be to have a bow thruster fitted, which gives you just that bit more manoeuvrability. This is basically a small propeller fitted below the waterline, used to push the bow to the left or right, reducing your dependence on the rudder.

Another key consideration will be the amount of deck space you prefer (and any compromises this may involve with interior space, more on this in Chapter 10) and the type of hull you will need. Most narrowboats are all steel; namely, the hull, sides and roof are all of the same material, welded together. Although sturdy and resilient, an all-steel boat can get

Classic 'trad' sterns.

Wide or narrow? It depends on your needs.

cold in winter and, as already mentioned, play havoc with mobile phone signals. Alternatives can include a steel hull with a wooden or fibreglass superstructure, and although lighter and possibly better insulated, their very manufacture requires a join where the top meets the bottom, and this then becomes a leak or draught risk. Of course, older boats may have a wooden hull, but whilst attractive, these require extra care and attention – think vintage car.

Whilst narrowboats do occasionally ride coastal waters this tends to be under highly controlled conditions and even then only in short bursts. Their flat-bottomed construction makes them simply unsuitable for the task, even if some highly publicised, and ill-advised, dashes across the English Channel to the French canals are sometimes made. Equally, large river and coastal-going craft will soon find that obstacles in the way of low bridges, locks and water depth will prevent them going too far inland.

If your choice is the canals and a narrowboat, these fall into three broad styles, defined in terms of the profile of the boat, with variations within these styles according to manufacturers, individual boatyards and local traditions.

The traditional 'trad' narrowboat has a small, unguarded deck at the back with the cabin far enough back for the helmsman to stand inside and protect the lower half of their body from the elements. The cruiser style takes its name from the river cruiser and has large open decks at the bow and stern whilst the third type is a compromise between the two, known perhaps inevitably as the 'semi-trad'. Like the cruiser style, the hatch and rear doors are placed forward but on the semi-trad the sidewalls continue from the sides to give more protected seating and a modicum of shelter for the helmsman. A further option, that is becoming quite popular, is the working boat, typically with roped canvas with portholes along the length of the boat, or a tug, and a long front deck useful for keeping motorcycles or bicycles with the space underneath being utilised for sleeping quarters.

As you might expect, the defining feature of a narrowboat is its lack of space, and whilst this may be regarded as cosy or romantic by outsiders, that view may be open to revision if you have to live in one for any length of time. As with most things, though, this can be seen as presenting problems or a set of challenges, and later chapters in this book provide ideas on how to meet these challenges, not least those of storage and internal layout.

The obvious solution to this fundamental flaw is to opt for a wider boat and accept that this may limit your cruising options. Alternatives include wide-beam boats, generally known as barges, although this term is often inaccurately also applied to narrowboats. Barges come in their own array of types but tend to have a beam of around 12ft and much higher decks. They can be either English, French or Dutch in style and were originally used for navigation on larger rivers.

Barges offer more room, but they are not that manoeuvrable, and may require a crew to get around. Their size can also present problems if you move your moorings regularly, and you are limited in how far inland you can progress, with rivers more barge-friendly than much of the canal network, with London, the Norfolk Broads and the rivers Severn and Trent particularly favourable, although the canal network around the Midlands can limit a north to south progression. As such, as a liveaboard option barges tend to be suitable if more than one person is involved and if you don't envisage moving around much.

Different types of barge were the result of different original uses, or from regional variations designed to meet specific local conditions. Often barges have their origins in boats capable of plying both the larger river navigations as well as near-coastal waters, bringing goods from inland to ocean-going ships.

Other unpowered, usually permanently moored boats (although they can be towed) include the traditional houseboat. These tend not to be distinguished by their style, with a functional rectangular construction on top of a hull the norm. None of your sleek lines here – houseboats have sometimes been compared to floating shipping containers converted into living space.

A further option for canal and river living is a fibreglass or GRP hull cruiser. These come in various sizes, ranging from the day boat right up to the ocean-going gin palace – often to be spotted inland on the Thames, although only as far as Oxford where the low Osney Bridge (7ft 6in headroom on a good day) tends to impede progress. Known disparagingly by some (mainly narrowboaters!) as 'plastic boats', these are cast from moulds and share many of the same problems of space with narrowboats. These boats are suitable for the Norfolk Broads and wider canals as well as most rivers, and are made to standard configurations. As such they are easier to specify and fit out and, if you are buying new, tend to be available much quicker than a narrowboat.

Lighter and easier to manoeuvre (they are typically powered by diesel or petrol outboard engines), cruisers also rock around more, and for many, cruisers seem less homely and more suited to short visits or day boating. That said, a small proportion of liveaboards manage to make their homes in them.

Motor cruisers are a larger version of this type, and are usually capable of sea crossings. When negotiating the speed-restricted inland waterways, they can give the appearance of powerful vessels stuck in first or second gear. Their more natural element is the coastal marina, where many do live on board them, although year-round living tends to be less popular as life on these boats can be uncomfortable in the winter, and such vessels are often lifted out of the water out of season. But not all cruisers are clean, shiny fibreglass, and it's possible to see oddities if you look in popular mooring spots, ranging from old motor torpedo boats through to lifeboats and every kind of craft made from wood, steel or even concrete!

Finally, if you do not expect to move, and you have somewhere to moor, your options suddenly multiply. Certain spots, with the Thames estuary a prime example, seem to act as magnets for large and at times quite eccentric craft which, if they ever floated, are unlikely to do so again. These are often more accurately described as houses built around a hull than boats converted into homes, which brings us onto our final set of decision-making criteria.

Houseboats can look more like a house than a boat.

House, Boat or Houseboat?

Having decided where you want to be and what type of craft you prefer, a conversation needs to take place about what exactly you are trying to achieve. Is your objective to replace your house with another living space that just happens to float? If you want to cruise, then considerations of safety probably mean you will want your craft to be a boat first and a home second. If you want to enjoy the pleasures of actually floating and not rule out the possibility of moving (although this would not be something you would expect to do too often), then you may wish to consider something in between – a houseboat.

Houseboats may or may not have an engine and tend to be highly functional in design, sometimes not really looking like a boat at all. As their name implies, these tend to fall more into the category of floating house rather than boat. In the eyes of the authorities houseboats tend to enjoy a more established status than other liveaboard craft, although the quid pro quo for this can be that they are obliged to congregate in designated spots where utilities and other basics of modern life highlighted in Chapter 1 are laid on. This state of near-permanence also reflects in the land beside them, which is often cultivated into a garden. This different status tends to set houseboats apart, a breed unto themselves and one perhaps not really 'of' the boating community – at least in some eyes.

Where to Start

Once you have weighed up all the various considerations discussed above and decided what sort of boat you're after, there is then the question of where to look for one. One option is to start from scratch, either by commissioning a boat from a builder or building (or more usually, fitting out) one on your own. This tends to be the most expensive way forward and the one that takes the most time, but it does mean that you are able to specify your requirements exactly. Starting from scratch tends to work best for those who have a very good idea of what it is they're after, usually because they are experienced liveaboards and have an excellent insight into their individual needs and expectations.

There is no shortage of boatbuilders willing to satisfy your needs and indeed to provide advice. Details can be gained from the boating press, with some magazines offering annual surveys of the industry, setting out areas of specific expertise. A word of warning here, however: in these straitened times many boatbuilders are finding it hard to make ends meet, so invest time in checking financial credentials before parting with any money. Building a boat takes time, so make sure your builder has the wherewithal to last the course. Alternatively, as suggested above, you may choose to acquire your own hull and get involved personally in fitting it out, first having found a friendly marina with access to the tools and other kit you may need. Another option may be to convert or adapt an existing craft, which may or may not have been used previously by a liveaboard. Clearly, the further you get away from working with a clean sheet, the tighter your room for manoeuvre will become, but you may find savings in both cost and time.

If your preference is to buy off the peg or second-hand you have two main options, assuming you do not already have your eye on a specific craft. The first is to buy off the page using one of the boating magazines or one of the growing number of websites offering boats for sale; the second is to go via a broker. Brokers tend to be based at the larger marinas and usually also have websites. These work on commission, but this is usually paid by the vendor, and going down this route does offer access to more advice and to services for checking any potential purchase out. Whilst vendors may be responsible for commissions, purchasers usually have to bear the cost of a survey, and having survey facilities on hand can help speed up the process. Stocks of boats at brokers tend to rise either at the beginning of 'the season', spring, or the end, when the first frost seems imminent; although demand for second-hand boats

has been running at an all-time high in recent years, driven in part by the growing numbers of liveaboards, which tends to reward those in a position to make quick decisions.

Be conscious always of the maxim 'buyer beware' – as the purchaser it is your responsibility to check out what you are buying, not the seller's to point out potential problems. Unlike cars, boats do not always come with a service history or logbook, although some may have some kind of proof of ownership, for example a bill of sale. Again, you may wish to make your own checks to make sure you are buying from the legal owner.

Whichever route you choose, be mindful of the golden rule: let the head rule the heart. An all too common tale involves potential liveaboards making the crucial decision of which boat to buy on the basis of minor details – the curtains, or the kind of stain used on the wood panelling. Even if you think you have found the boat you want – and remember this decision will inevitably involve compromise, as you will never find the perfect boat – pause before committing yourself and find time to examine and compare different boats, so you can appreciate the exact nature of the compromises you are prepared to make. At the same time, don't forget the basics. You wouldn't buy a car without taking it for a spin, and in the same way it's worth checking how a boat handles. Equally, when you finally find a boat that ticks all the main boxes, don't fall into the trap of assuming everything else works. Check electrical points, the galley, navigation lights, gas compartments and so on; finding out there's a list of minor niggles to sort out after you've acquired your new home can take the gloss off your purchase.

If you want to learn in more detail how to finance the purchase of a boat turn to Chapter 8, but in general terms, if you are commissioning a new boat the normal practice is to put down a deposit (10–20 per cent) and make staged payments at agreed points in the boat's construction. A first-stage payment might be at the point when the hull is complete, the second when the engine is fitted, and the third stage may be payable upon fitting out. This gives you the option to get a third-party opinion at different points in the boat's construction before handing over your hard-earned cash, but be aware of when these stages are coming up, as you may have to book ahead for a professional opinion and won't want to have work halted pending an inspection.

A good tip here is to work to a standard contract such as that offered by the British Marine Federation (www.britishmarine.co.uk), which has been designed to protect both the boatbuilder and the customer. Be sure also that all the requirements of the EU's Recreational Craft Directive (RCD) are fulfilled, as you will not get a Boat Safety Certificate (BSC) otherwise. If you go down the route of buying a narrowboat shell to complete yourself, the supplier of the shell also has to provide an RCD Annexe 3 Certificate and you won't need to comply with the RCD requirements unless you resell the boat within five years – although you will still be obliged to get a BSC. Given that these regulations change all the time, it is worth checking that no changes have been made since publication of this book, should this be your preferred option.

Choosing a boat is only the beginning of the liveaboard story. Just as important is what you do with it afterwards. Like householders, liveaboards like to customise their space and environment – and some are more diligent at maintenance than others. As such, the range of liveaboard boats is as varied as the people living on them.

Some assume the status of little palaces, following the rule of thumb that states that the amount of time spent beautifying a boat is inversely proportional to the time spent actually cruising – whatever one's initial intentions might have been. Others fall into disrepair, the ambition to 'do up' a boat being unequal to the sheer scale of the challenge. All this goes to prove that liveaboards are not such a different breed – just people.

A classic Dutch barge.

A good example of a broad-beam boat.

Although they can look impressive, wooden boats bring a lot of maintenance with them.

Questions for Choosing a Boat

▶ Do you intend to cruise or will your boat be permanently moored?

▶ What type of waterway do you want to be on?

  Canal?

  River?

  Coastal?

  Estuary?

▶ What type of boat do you want?

  Narrowboat?

  Broad beam?

  River cruiser?

  Barge?

  Houseboat?

  Something different?

▶ What size of boat do you want?

▶ Will you be alone?

▶ Do you expect to have pets?

▶ What can you and your crew manage?

▶ What type of mooring can you afford?

▶ Have you considered a houseboat?

CHAPTER 4

MOORINGS

Popular notions of the waterborne equivalent of the 'freedom of the road' carry a fair degree of truth, at least if you choose the canals. So long as you pay your licence you have considerable freedom to roam the vast majority of the UK's inland waterways. The point at which reality kicks in is when you have to stop for any length of time – either at a base or moorings – and, perhaps because it involves land, this is an area that has become increasingly bound up in regulations in recent years.

Liveaboards tend to fall into three broad categories. The first is what is called a 'continuous cruiser', a water nomad always on the move. Although they have no permanent mooring, this type of liveaboard is not immune to the need to stop every now and then, even if it's just for the night, and few continuous cruisers opt to stay moving in the dead of winter. Indeed, this choice is often made for them through the need for regular maintenance of the waterways conducted during planned stoppages. These tend to start in November and can carry on through to Easter, typically with a break over Christmas. Equally, it is not unknown for the canal to freeze over in particularly severe weather, and moving in these conditions is not advised, not least because even the thinnest layer of ice can have a scouring effect on the hull blacking of both your own boat and those of others you pass.

The second group may be termed the permanently moored liveaboard. These tend to have a home mooring where they spend most, if not all their time. The third lies somewhere between the two, let's call them the semi-permanent or seasonal cruiser, who may be on the move for much of the year but moor up for the winter, not necessarily always at the same place, or may even decamp to a shore-side base to see out the wind, rain and cold.

Moorings seem to be a contentious issue amongst the canal community, perhaps because there will always be a contingent who regard the inland waterways as belonging to the people, in much the same way some internet users resist any attempt to police cyberspace, and perhaps because of an inbuilt resistance to institutions, especially ones which effectively operate a monopoly.

Marinas remain a popular choice for liveaboards looking for a sense of community.

The Authorities

Before considering the different mooring options, it's worth pausing to consider who these institutions wielding authority are. Most of the inland waterways come under the remit of the Canal and River Trust (www.canalrivertrust.org.uk), a charity which came into existence in 2012 when it took on the responsibilities previously discharged by British Waterways (BW), which at the time was an arm of the Department for Environment, Food & Rural Affairs (DEFRA). The CRT is responsible for 2,000 miles of inland canals and rivers. Other inland rivers, including the Thames, Medway, Nene, Stour and Great Ouse, are the responsibility of the Environment Agency, whilst the Norfolk Broads, perhaps unsurprisingly, come under the Broads Authority. Other players include Scottish Canals, a body of the Scottish government, responsible for the canals in Scotland, the National Trust, responsible for the Wey Navigations, and the Manchester Ship Canal, which owns the Bridgewater Canal.

The circumstances of the CRT's formation and its subsequent remit are of interest here. Back in 2006, the Trust's predecessor BW was suddenly required to cut back substantially on its budget as a result of funding problems within its parent government department, DEFRA. At one point, this looked like posing a very real threat to the continued existence of the waterways. Disaster was averted, but the crisis led BW to put forward a proposal for it to enter the then fashionable 'third sector', namely a body independent of government, an idea also in tune with the coalition government's 'big society' ideology.

The proposal was the creation of an independent charitable trust, with a timescale to become financially independent, eradicating the £30 million budget deficit BW was then running. At the same time, the new body, which became the CRT, would strive to become more inclusive by involving all waterways users. A fundamental shift that resulted from this was a move away from being a government body towards being an autonomous trust, with a remit to make decisions based upon what it deems best rather than from a sense of obligation to specific users. This model has resulted in a not immediately reconcilable combination of more hard-headed commercial approach to those from whom it levies charges (almost exclusively boaters) and a 'softer' outward image. Given the need to walk this tightrope, it is hardly surprising that not everyone on the waterways, notably those who had grown used to an at times more laissez-faire, take-each-case-as-it-comes approach from BW, has embraced the CRT wholeheartedly, especially when it comes to issues connected with mooring.

Evidence of the continued contentiousness around mooring includes the fact that this was the subject of a major review by British Waterways between 2007 and 2011, and as a result, more spaces were made available in private marinas but places on the towpath (which tend to be cheaper) came under stricter control, both in numbers and how they are policed. The CRT has tended to maintain this more rigorous approach, in line with its shift to a greater sense of commerciality.

Continuous Cruisers

One area where the CRT has been noticeably active is also probably the one that generates the most controversy: continuous cruising. Traditionally, British Waterways took a relatively benign approach to enforcing mooring regulations with continuous cruisers, taking an approach characterised as 'let's all be sensible about this' and 'if you ask we may well say yes', even though increasing abuse of this attitude by a growing minority had led to the introduction of more defined rules about what they would and would not accept.

Whilst some latitude does still exist, for example in the case of illness or poor weather, continuous cruisers do well to stay within the spirit of the regulations and to foster good relations with the powers that be. Mooring wardens (yes they do exist!) tend not to be quite as tenacious as traffic wardens but they have the power to be if they so choose. In practice many mooring wardens are also fellow liveaboards, which can help.

To be defined as a continuous cruiser, and thereby exempt from the requirement to prove a permanent mooring, requires being able to demonstrate that your boat is being used for navigation throughout the period of a licence. In practice, this means the continuous cruiser needs to be able be prove they are 'moving, in passage or transit' throughout. This is interpreted as moving on from a spot within fourteen days, with 'a spot' defined as 'a neighbourhood', which itself is open to local interpretation.

The canny reader may spot an opportunity here to move back and forth between two spots or neighbourhoods, but the rules are clear that the cruiser needs to be moving 'from A to B to C to D rather than A to B to A to B'. Helpfully, the CRT suggests two questions a potential continuous cruiser needs to ask themselves. First, are you free of obligations that would see you having to remain in one area, such as children's education, employment or healthcare? Second, can you commit to moving your boat to a truly new area every fourteen days? The suggestion is that if you answer 'no' to either of these then you can't really regard yourself as a candidate to become a continuous cruiser.

This is perhaps the issue that generates the greatest friction between the CRT and the liveaboard community, reflected in both news stories and even the occasional demonstration. Whilst the rules and guidelines may be clear, these can come up against the realities on the ground, where gaining a permanent mooring can, in some areas, be all but impossible or unfeasible financially. On top of this, there is a perception amongst many in the liveaboard community that the CRT has taken an unnecessarily strict line on enforcement, even suggesting they will refuse to renew the licences of those who fall foul of their guidelines (and unlicensed boats can be seized and even destroyed), whilst the CRT would no doubt respond they are only doing their duty. This perception has in turn fed a feeling amongst some that the CRT wants to 'clean up' the canals, a view the CRT would probably refute, even if the perception persists.

The reality on the ground is that whereas there might have been some room for interpretation under the old regime, that was the past, and as such choosing the option to become a continuous cruiser is not one that should be taken lightly. Throughout, the burden of proof lies with the licence holder, so those who go down the continuous cruiser line are well advised to keep a log of their movements, just in case.

The continuous cruiser option is without doubt the most extreme for the possible liveaboard, and will suit only a particular type of personality and lifestyle. Many of the potential sacrifices associated with living on board a boat, including the less tangible and more psychological aspects associated with becoming a 'floating citizen', are most profound for those who take this route. Issues such as communications, access to services and whether or not you need to earn a living (even if a floating office makes this possible, remember that internet access is far from perfect with a moving boat) are all important considerations in making this choice.

Permanent Moorings

The permanently moored enjoy greater security and more facilities – if they are lucky, maybe even an address – which come with having a base, even if this does come at the price of less freedom. For those on rivers and canals there are basically two options for long-term moorings. Either you can stay at marinas and boatyards, or you can moor bankside, with the latter subdivided into towpath and non-towpath moorings.

Yes, mooring wardens do exist!

Marinas tend to offer better access to electricity.

Marinas tend to be privately owned and offer more facilities, ranging from semi-gated communities with a full range of facilities such as laundries, showers, Wi-Fi and a club house, as well as often having access to maintenance help, not to mention often high levels of security including CCTV, through to bases that barely deserve to be called marinas, being little more than a spare bit of space at a boatyard.

If you decide to go down the marina route, the choice is wide, and you'll be driven by where you want to be, the type of environment you are most comfortable in and the size of your wallet – for mooring in a marina is by far the most expensive option for the liveaboard. Furthermore, if you do decide to make a marina your home, you need to check first whether this is something that is encouraged, as some marinas are keener than others on having permanent residents. Some marinas explicitly ban residential moorings, whilst others have what may be termed a flexible approach, with individuals judged on a case-by-case basis.

Another consideration is whether you expect to be doing a lot of work to your boat. Few marina owners are happy when their facility begins to look like a construction site. In these cases a mooring attached to a boatyard is the better option, as not only do you have access to professional expertise, but boatyards are also better equipped to take deliveries of materials.

Finally, one recent development has been the sale of leasehold moorings (typically for thirty years), so that when a boat is sold its mooring can go with it. Whilst this does provide extra security it also comes with some risk attached. How do you know that the marina will remain in its current ownership for the duration of your lease? Also, if you ever want to sell your boat, is there any guarantee that the new owner will also want you to live in the marina?

Non-towpath or offside bankside mooring tends to be made available either by marinas, boatyards or cruising clubs. There are over 100 cruising clubs in the UK, grouped together under the umbrella of the Association of Waterways Cruising Clubs (www.awcc.org.uk), with many of them offering a berth to the liveaboard as well as an instant community to become part of. A useful guide on the subject of non-towpath moorings is *Getting Residential Moorings Right*, from the ROBA (Residential Boat Owners' Association) and London Rivers Association.

Offside mooring is also possible by buying or renting a strip of private land alongside a waterway, and although these are not cheap, they can be quite cost-effective compared with the alternatives, and especially if you are looking to moor in a city centre. Be warned though – good spots are usually snapped up as soon as they become available, and if you rely on picking one up through an advert you are likely to be disappointed. Instead you need to hook into the boating grapevine, with mooring wardens, other liveaboards and boatyard owners all good sources of information.

It is not possible simply to buy a strip of land and declare it a mooring, but that's not to say you cannot buy a strip of land and have it approved as a mooring. In the case of canals the water comes under the auspices of the CRT, whereas purchase of a strip of land alongside a river does bring with it certain riparian rights, including owning the water to the centre of the river. If you are looking to create a coastal mooring then you will need to gain permission from the Crown Estate.

Both the CRT and the Environment Agency like to pass approval on potential mooring sites and will charge you for the privilege, in the case of the former typically at half the rate of equivalent local moorings. The Environment Agency will also wish to ensure that a possible mooring will not represent a hazard in the event of a flood. The authorities also reserve the right to refuse you mooring status, for example if you are too close to a bridge or a lock or are likely to present a navigational hazard.

Until recently towpath, or online, moorings have been the most straightforward option for the liveaboard, assuming of course that this is permitted in the spot you have your eye on. On one level these offer the convenience of being able to access 'the system' easily, as well as being less expensive than the alternative, but they are likely to be less well endowed with facilities than, say, a marina. On the canals and rivers, towpath moorings are controlled by the relevant authorities, and the reality has been that towpath moorings have been much easier to obtain on canals than they are on rivers. That said, these moorings are subject to the laws of supply and demand, with the latter tending to outstrip the former. The CRT has a separate website listing its moorings, www.watersidemooring.com, although it is worth remembering that the sites they control represent only a very small minority of the total.

Until recently BW operated on a 'waiting list' principle, but this is another area where the CRT has tended to show a more hard-nosed approach in recent years. Whilst BW's approach had the benefit of fairness, in reality it meant that the newcomer could wait for years to access their desired mooring spot. In its latter days, BW moved towards a sealed bid auctioning system, an approach the CRT has stuck with, to the dismay of many who feel that the thickness of one's wallet should not be the prime criterion for allocating scare resources.

At the same time there seems to have been a mood shift in the recent past away from online moorings, which are felt to have become too congested in certain places – a consideration when other users are required to slow down when passing moored boats. Long stretches of residential-only mooring can also, perhaps inevitably, take on a dishevelled air over time, with liveaboards felt to be colonising the towpath meant for the enjoyment of all. Inspections, backed up by sanctions, have become a more frequent feature of towpath liveaboard life, part of a wider 'gentrification' of the waterways perhaps. Increasingly, liveaboards are being encouraged through force of circumstance to seek either a non-towpath base or locations that are off the beaten track, such as disused arms or basins.

But at whatever cost it comes, a permanent bankside mooring does offer the opportunity for that most innocent of an Englishman's pleasures: his garden. Being closer to nature tends to bring out the gardener in even the least green-fingered boater, and rare is the liveaboard who doesn't make at least some attempt to grow some of their own food (even if it's just a few herbs) or to adorn their boat with flowerpots. Often these line the top of the roof and, although attractive, they can cause excessive rusting if not protected. A rough rule of thumb suggests that the more pots a boat has, the less it travels, with the pots offering both tangible and intangible evidence of roots having been laid down.

This gardening instinct is less easy to satisfy in a marina, probably because boats are more likely to be moored alongside pontoons, or because there is less sense of permanence in a marina. Bankside mooring does offer this opportunity, even if it is curtailed somewhat if you choose a towpath mooring.

Finally on the issue of canal-side moorings, before selecting a location it is worth checking some of the things you cannot see, such as the depth of the water and whether the bed is regularly dredged. How often is the bankside vegetation cut? Other issues worth thinking about include how easy it might be to dispose of rubbish and your access to sanitary facilities and a water point. On all these issues, the best source of information by far is people who are already in the vicinity.

Permanent riverside moorings are much harder to come by than those on the canals, and potential liveaboards planning to live by a river have to secure their berth before they buy their boat. It has been estimated that a boat roughly triples in value if it has a permanent residential mooring, so long as the tenure is for at least ten years. These do not come cheap, however, and like everything the more desirable it is the more it will cost,

Tidal moorings bring their own considerations, such as the need for a floating gangway.

A line of 'offline' moorings, with the towpath just visible to the right.

with the best running into thousands of pounds a year, or even more in the heart of London.

Finally, tidal moorings come with their own complexities and the best source of information on these is The Yacht Harbour Association (www.tyha.co.uk). In short, tidal moorings tend to fall into classifications that indicate how easy they are to get away from. A mud berth is a mooring that dries out when the tide recedes, leaving your boat sitting on mud, which can make access difficult if you are not tied up to a jetty and can bring with it related problems, not least the smell of the mud.

Some tidal moorings may be classified as +/- two hours HW, meaning that you can move your boat two hours either side of high water. Others may be termed Half Tide moorings, whereby your boat can be moved for half the tide, or All States of Tide, which is self-explanatory. Boats will rise and fall with the tide. Flat-bottomed boats need to sit on bearers so the incoming water can get underneath the boat or it may stay down as a vacuum forms between the bottom of the boat and the mud below. At low tide such boats may become inaccessible.

Semi-Permanent Moorings

Semi-permanent moorings can offer a potential 'win-win' to both landowners and those whose liveaboard status may vary with the seasons. If you are a semi-permanent cruiser, i.e. out on the water on a 'continuous voyage' for part of the year but holed up on dry land for the rest of the year – an increasingly popular option amongst retired people who may have a property abroad or swapped their family home for a more convenient flat – then you still need somewhere to leave your boat in the off season, exactly the time that boatyards are keen to generate some extra income and when less traffic means its possible to juggle more boats in the same space. The CRT sometimes provides winter moorings from October to March using summer visitor moorings and it is normally worth checking to see if there are any available in your area. Another option for this breed is to own a property which has its own water frontage, although remember that the authorities will need to sanction its use as a mooring (see above).

The advice given above represents the official line. However, as may be becoming clear by now, within this there does remain some room for what might be called 'interpretation' on the ground. Although often demonised, the waterways authorities exist to serve their customers and their representatives on the ground may often take a more pragmatic

Permit
Holders
Only

view of what is and is not acceptable in a particular locality. Although they would never admit it, it is not unknown for them to turn the occasional blind eye to situations, which may have existed for years or are doing no one any real harm. This cannot be relied upon to continue, however, and it is fair to say that regulations have been more firmly enforced in recent years. That said, our waterways and coasts represent many thousands of miles with all sorts of nooks and crannies capable of harbouring the whole range of life afloat!

Left: A convenient mooring for the office?

Centre: Types of mooring tend to be clearly marked.

Right: Mooring in a built-up area can present its own challenges.

Questions for Moorings

> **?** Do you need a permanent base?

> **?** Are you a likely to be a continuous cruiser, someone needing a permanent mooring or a semi-permanent mooring?

> **?** What range of facilities do you value most?

> **?** Where's the nearest water point?

> **?** If you are considering a bankside mooring, consider how the immediate vicinity may change with the seasons – will it get muddy or flood for instance?

> **?** Are there existing liveaboards where you are considering mooring? Talk to them and ask them about the good and bad things about living there.

> **?** How close are the shops and other non-immediate facilities?

> **?** Will you want access to other transport? What is public transport like? Is there somewhere to leave a car/motorbike/bike safely if need be?

> **?** Is there any history of vandalism or theft on a mooring or in a marina?

CHAPTER 5

HEATING, COOKING AND SANITATION

The clearest divide between liveaboards and leisure boaters is probably the seasons. Whilst leisure boaters can dream of gliding gently along the waterways with the sun to their back, accompanied by baby ducklings and the sound of beer bottles opening, liveaboards know that in time the seasons will change and with it the cold and wet will return. It is essential, therefore, to make sure that your boat is a holiday caravan that just happens to be able to move under its own steam, but is also capable of taking all that the great British climate can throw at it. In addition, holiday boaters always have the option of restricting their use of the on-board galley to breakfasts and the odd cuppa, and know that they only have to 'put up with' the toilet arrangements for a week or possibly two. This chapter therefore considers three of the most basic areas that differentiate the liveaboard from the tourist: heating, cooking and sanitation.

Insulation

Very little separates the boater inside their boat from the elements always battling to get in from the outside. A vital, but usually unseen and therefore too often unregarded, determinant of future comfort is insulation. Good insulation should be able to keep you warm in the winter and cool in the summer.

If you are in the happy position of choosing what form of insulation your boat has, you will need to balance considerations of efficiency (measured in terms of its K-value: the lower the value, the more efficient it is), its bulk (you have limited space to play with so you don't want to use it up with something you won't see) and finally its cost. If you are fitting your own insulation you may also wish to consider how easy or difficult it may be to fit, and even if you aren't, this will have an impact upon the cost of fitting it – although it should be stressed that good insulation is one of those areas it isn't worth stinting on; it's very difficult to fix afterwards. If you are buying a second-hand boat, put asking about the insulation on your checklist, remembering that a boat built primarily for spring to autumn hiring may not have quite the insulation levels you will need if you are going to live on board all year round.

Good insulation is essential if you are going to brave all the seasons on board.

There are five main types of insulation material, the relative merits of which are summarised in the table opposite. A key factor in determining a good insulation material is whether or not it allows moisture to form behind it, as dampness here will slowly attack both wood and metal and rot the superstructure from the inside. The five types are:

Spray Foam

Polyurethane foam applied in a spray, which then expands. This material bonds to metal or wood and its closed-cell structure means it is impermeable to moisture. This is the most common insulation applied to newer narrowboats and until recently could only be applied by specialist contractors, although recent advances in technology are now enabling DIY kits to be produced.

Foam Boards

These can be comprised of polystyrene, polyurethane or polyisocyanurate foam pre-applied to boards for ease of fitting. The boards are cut to size and attached to battens, although the cutting can be a precision job if you are not to waste a lot. Boards are more DIY friendly, needing less specialist equipment, but getting a tight fit is essential and they need to be vapour sealed.

Rockwool

Available in batts (a compressed version that looks a bit like a board) or rolls. This is the sort of insulation seen in most house lofts. Rockwool is easily applied, although it too has to be vapour sealed. Cheaper than the alternatives, Rockwool is only around half as efficient as foam and will therefore take up more of your precious space. Rockwool can be applied by the amateur but needs to be handled with care because the fibres it is made up from require the use of masks and gloves.

Thinsulate

Available in rolls, this too can be fitted by the amateur by cutting it to size, gluing it into place and vapour sealing to avoid gaps. Thin but expensive, Thinsulate also has a relatively poor K-value, on a par with Rockwool.

Expanded Polystyrene

This tends to be found in older boats and must be fireproofed before use. Where this material is used, PVC wires have to be run through conduits as continuous contact rots the insulation. Expanded polystyrene used to be inexpensive, which explains its previous popularity.

Relative Merits of Different Insulation Materials

Material	Bulk	Cost	Efficiency	Ease of Installation
Spray Foam	Medium	Medium	Medium	Best done by a specialist
Foam Boards	Medium	Medium	Medium	Medium but time-consuming
Rockwool	High	Low	Medium	Medium
Thinsulate	Low	High	High	Medium
Expanded Polystyrene	Low	Low	Low	Medium

Other areas of potential heat loss are the windows, floors and doors. Double glazing is a serious option for liveaboards, offering the twin advantage of keeping heat in and noise out. It is not cheap though, usually requiring sealed units to be made, with retrofitting often very difficult (although easier for portholes). Heat is also lost through doors and ventilation holes and although there is little that can be done about the latter, some basic insulation around the doors can reward the effort involved.

Heating

Assuming you have made your boat as snug as possible, a good heating system is essential, not only to keep yourself warm but also to stop the boat freezing up and to keep it dry. In the height of summer it's often difficult to imagine how vulnerable your living space is to the cold, especially water pipes and anything else that contains water, such as pumps and water heaters. The boater has two main options on heating. The first is a central heating system and the second involves some kind of solid fuel stove. Central heating requires a boiler and this can be either gas or diesel fuelled, while solid fuel tends to be wood, some form of coal, or a mix of the two.

There are few things more depressing than returning from a spell away to a cold damp boat with cold damp sheets and cold damp clothes hanging in the wardrobe. The speed with which your system can heat up your boat, combined with the need to keep Jack Frost at bay while you are away, can, therefore, be deciding factors when considering which option to go for. Central heating can be left on 'tick over', whilst solid fuel tends to be either on or off. Whether you expect to be away from your boat much in the winter – if it is cold, even just for a day at a time – is therefore a factor in deciding which way to go. It may also help to lag certain pipes, although if you suffer any damage it will inevitably be the one area you didn't protect!

It is worth remembering at this point that other features of a boat will also generate warmth, such as an inboard engine if you have one, the cooker, fridge and, not least, the people living on it, but these are unlikely to be enough on their own to keep you comfortable. The engine has to be running to generate heat, as does the fridge, although the colder months are likely to be the times when you are using these the least – indeed some liveaboards choose to turn their fridges off altogether in the winter to save electricity, it being just as sensible to keep food suspended from the pole outside.

Gas central heating typically involves an Alde-type boiler run off the gas bottle. These have the advantage of offering more-or-less instant heat and hot water, although they do accelerate your consumption of gas, so having easily accessible gas storage becomes a necessity, especially if you are going to be changing bottles in the cold. Alternatively, boilers can be diesel-fuelled, typically with a feed line from the main diesel tank, and some diesel-fired boilers are made to look like a traditional stove, giving them an added advantage.

Diesel boilers offer the same advantages as gas but do need regular servicing and de-coking, a job that can be messy, which is a particular consideration when you have to do it in what is effectively your front room. Also popular are diesel-fired heaters such as Eberspächer, Webasto and Mikuni, but these need regular servicing which tends to be very expensive. Diesel heating systems also need to be checked to ensure they are designed for regular rather than occasional use – another item for the checklist if you are buying second-hand, remembering that leisure boats tend to be used during the months when heating is less of a requirement.

Central heating does not come without its own problems. Systems need an electric circulation pump, and if the batteries run flat and this stops working, there is a risk that water may start to boil in the tank. They also need a header tank at the highest point and this isn't always something that is easy to achieve on a boat. Finally, systems need to be topped up with anti-freeze to avoid corrosion and to avoid the possibility of freezing pipes in the winter. Boilers can be plumbed into the hot water tank, which in turn may be kept warm using the engine cooling water via a calorifier.

Solid-fuel stoves come in various shapes and sizes and though they don't offer the same kind of instant heat, on the surface they may seem the simpler (and cheaper) option. But they can be difficult to regulate once blazing, and many a boater has fired up a solid-fuel stove only to find

A diesel heater.

Gas canisters are readily available and are the main fuel of choice for most liveaboards.

Coal stocked up and ready for the winter.

themselves sitting in their underwear or opening windows and doors to get back to a comfortable environment after an hour or so! Solid-fuel stoves can also be used to heat water through a back boiler.

The most efficient place to locate a solid-fuel stove is in the centre of the boat, although this is not always practical. One way round this is to install a heat-operated fan on top of the stove to circulate the heat. A number of efficient models are now on the market, although even the best model is unlikely to send heat to the extremes of a 60ft or 70ft boat.

When it comes to fuel, wood tends to burn faster than coal, but whatever you use needs to be stored somewhere, either on the roof or on the towpath if you have storage. Wood can generally be foraged for if you are on the move regularly, and as such offers a considerable cost advantage – once you have invested in the necessary chopping equipment and muscle power.

If using wood, you should make sure that you clean the chimney regularly, as tar builds up and blocks the flue. There are many brands of solid fuel with the most popular being Taybright, although Barge Nuts are also popular. Other types of fuel are Anthracite, Excel, Phurnacite and Homefire Ovals, although for the sake of the environment and out of respect for your neighbours you should always use smokeless fuel. Along some stretches of waterway, solid fuel can be bought from canal traders selling from their boats.

Stoves are also necessarily messy. Although most have ash cans for (relatively) convenient removal, if you are stationary you will need somewhere to deposit the ash (which may be hot when you want to get rid of it). Another thing to bear in mind with solid fuel in particular is the need for adequate ventilation and a good carbon monoxide detector. Possible carbon monoxide poisoning is not restricted to solid-fuel stoves, as the gas is a by-product of the combustion of any carbon-based fuel including diesel and gas, and all boaters should be alert to the possible signs and symptoms. These include so-called 'lazy' flames – ones that seem to be struggling to stay alight – and physical symptoms such as irritated eyes, headaches, nausea and dizziness – some of which can easily be mistaken for seasickness or alcohol intoxication. Carbon monoxide is sometimes known as the 'silent killer' and the gas can accumulate in areas such as the engine compartment. The threat it poses must always be taken seriously.

Whilst on the subject of safety, it probably goes without saying – but we'll say it anyway – that solid-fuel stoves do represent a very real fire hazard. Anything flammable should be kept well away from them – not something that's always easy in a confined space. The surrounding area, namely the back and sides of the fire, should be lined behind the tiles with Asbestolux or the equivalent, and there should be some form of hearth in the front of the fire to catch the glowing embers. They also need to be well secured and ventilated, with most having a detachable chimney on the outside of the boat, although it is all too easy to forget that the chimney inside will also get very hot!

But for the experienced liveaboard, a solid-fuel stove can be a friend, offering a visible source of comfort as well as a place to keep food warm (or even to cook it in the first place) as well as somewhere to dry gloves, socks and other small items. Given the various advantages and disadvantages offered by different heating options, it is perhaps unsurprising that many boaters go for a mixed system, combining the practicalities of central heating with the romanticism of a solid-fuel fire. This has the added advantage of removing reliance on one system, making sure you have a way of staying warm if one element fails.

Cooking

When it comes to cooking, the most popular option is gas, although diesel cookers are becoming more popular. Electric cookers are also used, though only where it is possible to hook up to an external power supply. In most cases electric ovens and hobs will prove too power-hungry, and for the same reason, most boaters will boil their water on a gas hob rather than use electric kettles.

The type of cooker fitted to a boat will depend on the type of boat it is. Wide-beamed boats such as Dutch barges may even have their own Aga-type stove, using either oil or solid fuel, whilst boats on a tidal mooring will tend to have gimballed stoves capable of swivelling to keep them level when the sea gets rough. Regulations dictate that a gas cooker needs to be fitted with a flame failsafe device, as otherwise if the flame blows out the unburned gas could end up in the bilges where it will wait for a spark to ignite it.

Cooking is of course another potential hazard, and the galley area needs to be well designed and thought out, as well as being provisioned with safety features such as fire extinguishers and fire blankets. A final point worth noting may not seem obvious and is worth pointing out: sink drain pipes should be as large a bore as possible and without a trap, as these tend to block up and smell. Finally, remember all waste water runs into the river or canal so you should use environmentally friendly washing-up liquid and soap powder such as those made by Ecover.

Sanitation

Sanitation is perhaps the most basic function of all and one you will want to get right! It is also possibly the aspect of life that is most different on a boat. In a house when you flush your toilet you flush your troubles away, but on a boat this is only the beginning of the story, and your 'troubles' stay with you until you dispose of them.

There are a number of options when it comes to a boat toilet and you may find your choice limited by how you choose to live. A static boat, for example, will by definition find it difficult to access external pump-out facilities, although this does not necessarily rule out the pump-out option, as we shall see. A good idea can also be to fit solar-powered fan-assisted vents in your toilet/shower.

Unlike some European countries, canal and river craft in the UK are not allowed to discharge into the waters they ply – thank goodness – and so have to be equipped with some kind of holding tank. Traditionally this has meant either cassette or pump-out toilets, although more recently a third option, composting toilets, has come onto the scene. Toilet design owes a lot to the camping and caravan industry, with built-in toilets a relatively modern innovation. For early boaters, a spade and some open ground had to suffice!

Cassette toilets, or, as they are sometimes known, Elsan or Porta Potti toilets, collect the waste in a cassette for disposal and involve the use of concentrated chemicals to keep odours at bay and allow multiple use before an opportunity arises for disposal. These chemicals, known as 'Blue', have a large amount of formaldehyde in them to kill off the anaerobic bacteria and also contain a large quantity of perfume, for obvious reasons. Formaldehyde is not a pleasant substance and should not come into contact with the skin. Alternatives do exist, including a substance known as 'Green', although these are of variable quality.

There are three basic types of cassette toilet: a simple plastic type with a self-contained water supply and a bowl and tank that clip together; a more sophisticated version with a plastic, floor-mounted toilet with an integral tank, which requires a trap door behind or at the side of the toilet to remove the cassette; and a third type which uses a vacuum, allowing the cassette to be fitted as far as 20ft away. These offer the added advantage of taking some of the odour away with them.

Cassette systems are cheap and simple, although they do have a limited storage capacity, which means you are advised to take opportunities for emptying whenever they come along, using designated sites. The issue

A diesel stove.

An Aga and a gas stove side by side.

Elsan disposal points are dotted along the waterways.

of access can be a problem too and most boaters, certainly liveaboards, choose to keep a spare cassette, which can be a storage problem.

Pump-out toilets are very simple in concept. They work on a gravity discharge basis; that is, the waste falls straight into a holding tank, which then needs to be emptied using a vacuum hose, hence the term pump out. Odour is again controlled using 'Blue', although not to the same levels. An alternative which some people find successful is to use live yeast. That said, smells can be a problem with both types of toilet, with the secret lying in frequent emptying and good disinfectant.

Pump-outs have the benefit of offering longer between emptying and the opportunity to give the tank a good old clean using fresh water. It should usually be possible to keep a holding tank clean, although some people just don't like the thought of sleeping with up to a month's worth of waste on board! Those with pump-out toilets have to be very careful about what goes down the pan, but having a 'proper' china pan is regarded as one of the benefits of a pump-out toilet.

The old adage that nothing should go into the tank that hasn't been eaten first is a good one, with even toilet paper sometimes being known to clog a pump-out system. Unclogging a pump-out is possible, but not particularly pleasant. Some pump-out toilets also have macerators or vacuums to allow the tank to stand a distance away from the pan, and these may also require less water for flushing. Macerators chop up solids and paper but will jam or break if any other object is put down the toilet. Their advantage is that the waste can be pumped through a small-bore pipe to a holding tank anywhere in the boat.

Pump-outs require a pump-out station, usually attached to marinas, although there are some self-service facilities, particularly on rivers. Pump-outs can become expensive, and just because a guide says a pump-out facility exists at a certain spot, this cannot be relied upon, as they tend to break down frequently and are repaired less frequently. This has led to an increase in demand for 'self-pump-out' pieces of kit, which vary from hand-pumped versions through to electronic machines, both feeding a tank that then has to be emptied.

A well-fitted pump-out toilet will be fitted with a gauge so that you can tell when you are close to needing a pump-out. There are few things worse on a boat than passing a pump-out facility and then finding out you needed it after all, with the next one two days away! As such, when the time for a pump-out is approaching, it's a wise boater who takes the first working facility available. A final consideration is to avoid pump-out outlets on the roof if possible, as most pumps do not really have enough suction to cope with the extra height.

Compost toilets have recently come into vogue, although these are still very much in their infancy. These are water-free and require a constant supply of electricity to make them work. The waste needs to be aerated on a daily basis, with the electricity powering a small fan to keep odours at bay. Water evaporates away, although there is some evidence that current systems do not allow this to happen fast enough, resulting in unpleasant smells. If you are thinking of having a drinking party on board and have a compost toilet, some kind of secondary backup is probably a good idea! Furthermore, current designs tend to be bulky and not that attractive to look at. On the upside, a correctly functioning compost toilet will require emptying only once a year, representing a considerable saving, although you may pay in other ways!

Whilst on the subject of 'green' solutions, given their unique need to live as close to self-sufficiency as practicable, liveaboards are potentially in an excellent position to take advantage of the new eco-friendly technologies now coming on stream. Opportunities may even exist to be pioneers of some of these new technologies, with solar power and recycling both good examples. Perhaps the area with the greatest potential is around water, a resource the permanent boater soon learns to value. Manufacturers of most current systems fitted to boats view water as a land-based householder might – as something disposable and of little value – while research into ways of reusing grey water generated on board a boat may pay dividends.

Self pump out kits can be very useful in case a disposal point you were relying on is out of commission.

A smoking chimney – all's well with the world!

Heating, Cooking and Sanitation

> How well insulated is your boat? If you are buying a second-hand boat check the material used and its K-value. If buying new make a balance between costs, bulk, efficiency and ease of application.

> How often do you expect to leave your boat in the winter? Do you need a trickle of heat and do you need to lag pipes?

> How long are you prepared to wait to heat up your boat and water? Do you need a boiler, and if so do you want it to be gas or diesel fuelled?

> If you opt for a gas boiler, how convenient are your spare bottles and how close are you to a gas stockist?

> If you opt for a diesel boiler, how happy are you about maintenance?

> If you opt for solid fuel, where will you keep stocks of wood and coal, and do you have somewhere you can dispose of ash?

> Do you have adequate safety precautions, especially carbon monoxide detectors, fire extinguishers and blankets?

> Is the galley near to the dining area?

> Is there good access to the sink and cooker?

> If going for a pump-out sanitation system, how convenient are facilities for pumping out, and have you factored the cost into your calculations?

> If going for a cassette-based sanitation system have you considered ease of access and storage room for a spare/used cassette?

Right: Is your craft also your lifeboat from the modern world?

Below: Foraged wood is often a good indicator there's a liveaboard inside.

Above: Cooking rabbit over an open fire.

Left: A plant trough waiting for the growing season.

Right: Urban living can be quite communal.

Below: If you can't have a garden, why not take one with you?

Right: Rural living gives more scope to 'spread out'.

Below: A matching pair?

Right: Each to their own!

Below: Everything in its place.

Right: A towpath garden.

Below: There's a boat in there somewhere!

Above: City centre living.

Right: You can even go to work by water.

Above: A Humber keel.

Left: Boats and flats cheek by jowl.

Right: A semi-trad narrowboat.

Below: Urban houseboats.

Right: A vibrant towpath display.

Below: A wide-beam barge, handy for the allotment.

Above: If you miss having a lawn, you can always take one with you.

Left: Typical narrowboat stoves.

Above: A foldaway trolley can save a lot of effort.

Left: A well-appointed narrowboat galley.

Right: A little touch of luxury.

Below: A gimballed oil lamp.

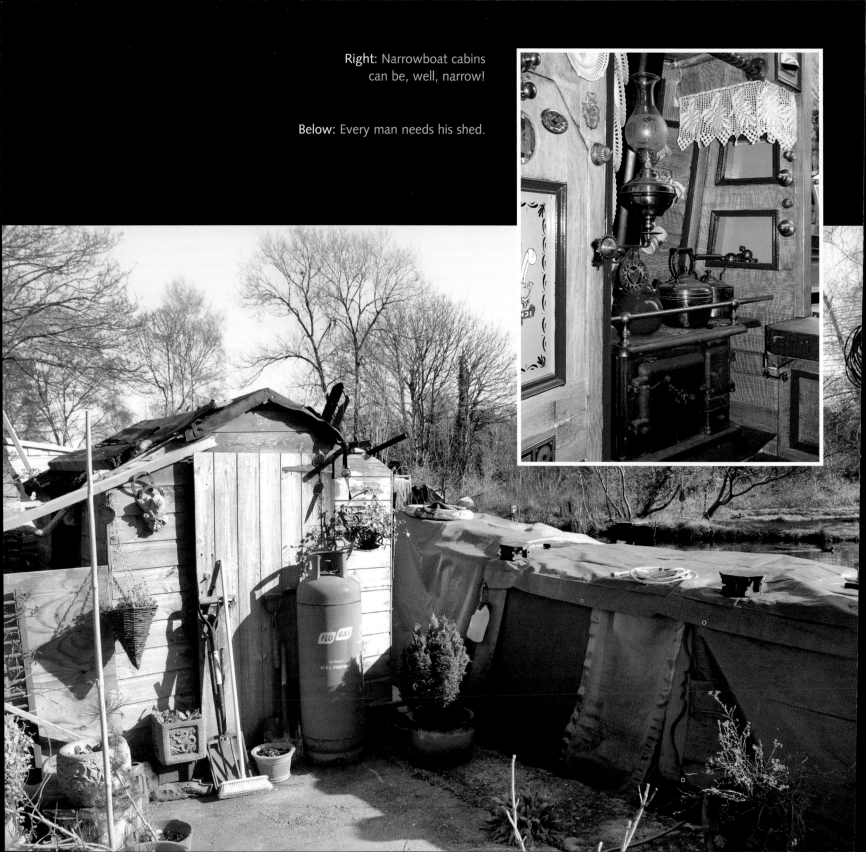

Right: Narrowboat cabins can be, well, narrow!

Below: Every man needs his shed.

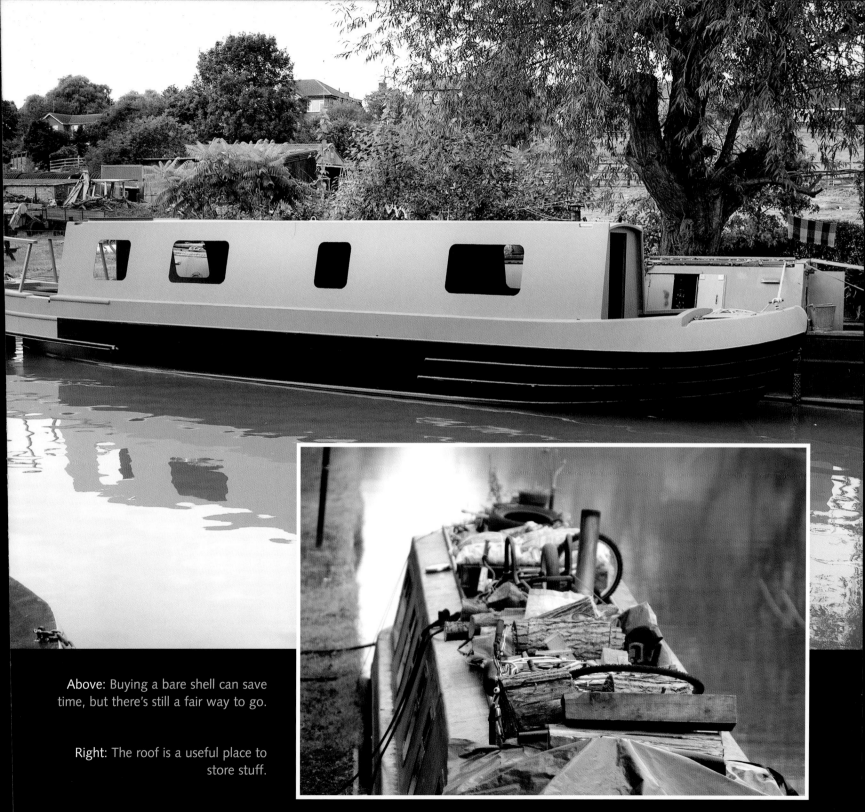

Above: Buying a bare shell can save time, but there's still a fair way to go.

Right: The roof is a useful place to store stuff.

Top: There's no need to miss your favourite programmes.

Above: Your stove is your friend in the winter.

Left: A GPS navigation system, suitably guarded.

Right: A good panel can help you monitor electricity generation and consumption.

Far right: Windpower can provide a useful top-up.

Below: Solar panels need to be taken down when on the move.

Above left: The stern tube greaser is easily forgotten, but vital.

Above: Boat–based businesses come in all guises, from this bike-hire boat ...

Left: ... to cafes ....

THE CANDY BOAT
SHOP

Above: … to sweets.

Left: Make sure you use a dry dock that is truly dry, like this one.

Right: From left to right, a conventionally blacked hull, a Zinga-coated hull and a steel-primed hull.

Below: Sometimes a boat just has to be lifted out.

Above: Sometimes you may need to call in the professionals.

Above right: Neglected paintwork will always come back to haunt you.

Right: Painting requires patience, as well as the right kit, materials and environment.

B.W. Nº 503128

Above: It's usually worth getting a professional to provide the finishing touches.

Right: Bikes should ideally be secured to the roof while you're away.

Left: Dogs are popular pets for liveaboards, but be selective on the breed.

Below: There are even floating churches.

Left: Doing your own painting is time-consuming, but can save a lot of cash.

Below: Remember – although you may live by yourself, you are part of a wider community.

LIFESTYLES AND LAYOUTS

The ideal layout of a liveaboard boat needs to reflect its occupants' lifestyle, and as everyone's lifestyle is different, so too will ideal layouts be different. The problem is that there's only a finite number of things you can do in the restricted space offered by a boat, and much of that is taken up by all the essentials discussed in previous chapters such as the engine and your life-support mechanisms, without which it's impossible to have any lifestyle at all!

The liveaboard therefore quickly learns a new respect for space if they are not to make too many compromises and thus defeat the point of becoming a liveaboard in the first place. And here lies the crux. Many of those seeking to become a liveaboard do so because they are looking for a shift in how they live their life – it is after all a fairly radical decision. As such, 'normal' determinants shouldn't be allowed to dictate one's lifestyle afloat, and priorities will inevitably change. Those who try to make the transition thinking they will simply replicate how they lived onshore, albeit perhaps scaled down a little, are almost certainly condemning themselves to failure. A fresh mindset is needed; one that relishes the opportunities and freedoms that living aboard offers, rather than fights it.

Those used to living in a house with a garden, a shed, an attic and maybe even a junk room can become blasé about space – which a liveaboard can never do. Before opting to become a liveaboard, it can be useful to look around your house and redefine what you regard as essential items, and the opportunity to embrace de-cluttering. Ask not 'what do I want?' but instead 'what do I need?'. Recalibrate what constitutes a necessity and what is actually a luxury.

In practical terms a key consideration here is practicality, usually a delicate balance between size, utility, whether any power is required to make it function (and if so how much) and ease of storage. Even items you may currently regard as basics, such as a vacuum cleaner or an ironing board, may be called into question, and that's long before you get onto thinking about the microwave, the coffee machine and the bread maker.

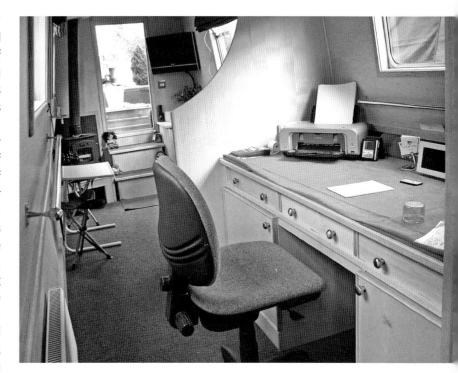

Do you need a dedicated office? This one cannily converts into a bed for guests.

One solution to the need for extra storage space …

This is where considerations of each individual's lifestyle come into play. If your life isn't worth living without freshly baked bread, what are you prepared to trade in order to get it? A good place to start is a cold analysis of what you really do need in order to function. Those who are still working and need to be smartly turned out every day may place a higher value on that ironing board as well as hanging wardrobe space – and don't forget that an electric iron is a very high consumer of electricity.

If you are semi-retired or intend to telecommute from your boat, or indeed have become a 'silver surfer' who finds technology the ideal way to keep in touch with children and grandchildren, then some kind of office with a computer will be high up on your list of priorities, as well a means of communicating with the outside world. Do you like to entertain? Do you have pets? Do you play a musical instrument? All these are considerations.

Boat Layout Basics

With the exception of houseboats and early narrowboats, water craft are not really designed to be lived on all year round, and indeed, those who originally lived on working narrowboats did so in an age of very different expectations, having to manage (and often even bring up a family) with a living space barely larger than a small tent. This is not to say that creating a desirable living space isn't possible; in fact there is now plenty of knowledge available on what does and doesn't work on boats which, when combined with further intelligence gleaned from the caravanning community, allows the potential liveaboard to construct pretty much whatever they want. The trick is plugging into that knowledge and matching it to your needs.

For reasons explored elsewhere in this book, narrowboats tend to be the most popular vessels for the potential inland waterways liveaboard, and although many of the hints and tips outlined here apply equally to other types of craft, the rest of this chapter will focus on them. The choice of craft has already been covered in Chapter 3, but to this should be added a mention of not only a boat's interior space, but also its exterior; after all, a 55ft trad style will have more interior space, but less exterior storage, than the same length cruiser style.

Decks and outside storage need to be factored into any decisions – having a secure cratch cover for example may mean that what may previously have been considered 'dead' space may be converted into 'live' storage, although with a diminished sense of security. Decks and roofs can also be used to store awkward items such as bikes or even small mopeds or garden furniture. Equally, if you are not constrained by the heights of bridges it may be possible to add extra 'stories', with some houseboats having a second floor and larger river craft more than one deck level.

Assuming you have decided on what type of boat you want and have your hull and insulation sorted out, your next decision is probably the interior finish. There are basically three options for wall covering: wood, paper or fabric, although not all these options may be available on a fibreglass or GRP cruiser.

Wood has the advantage of offering a warm feel and traditional look as well as a wide range of finishes, from light oak or ash to the darker mahogany or teak, with the lighter shades tending to be less claustrophobic. Wood panelling may be tongue-and-groove or veneered onto ply or blockboard, with hardwood used for detailing, or for window and door surrounds. An alternative is to use plain pine, although this tends to be less popular these days, perhaps because it darkens with age and can be a fire hazard near a chimney or stove.

Walls can also be finished with fabric, in a variety of styles. The walls can either be completely finished in this way, or just from the gunwale up, or one can carpet the walls from the gunwale down, which adds to the insulation of the boat and has the added advantage of being cheap. Walls may also be painted or papered, although the latter tends to be more common in houseboats. Similar options exist for ceilings.

When it comes to floor coverings there are four main options. Carpet tiles are a popular choice, being hard-wearing and easy to replace – although it is always a good tip to buy extras when you first fit them, as getting exact replacements afterwards is not always easy. Fitted carpets need to be laid by a professional and, as is often the way, you get what you pay for. There will be clear paths through the boat which will be trodden much more frequently than others and so hardiness will be important, as will ease of cleaning – it will not always be possible to change into carpet slippers every time you need to walk through. It is also worth fitting insulation under carpets, since after all, your floor level is below the waterline.

Wooden floors are also favoured for their durability and general utility and are an especially good idea if you have a dog. They can stain if allowed to stay wet, however, and can be damaged by heavier types of footwear (and heels) as well as having the potential to get extremely slippery when wet. Floor tiles are also an option. These can be cold to bare feet first thing in the morning though, and a rug secured with non-slip tape is highly recommended. Finally, vinyl flooring has its place in the galley and bathroom areas, and again a non-slip variety is a good idea. These have the virtue of cleaning easily and being extremely hard-wearing.

.... although this may be more practical (so long as low bridges don't get in the way!).

A galley may end up looking very similar to a house kitchen, just a bit more compact.

Now you have the basic interior decided, you need to think about how to split it up into different rooms. In theory you can divide your space however you want to, but inevitably there are practical constraints, some of which are touched on elsewhere, such as the position of the engine, location of the boiler and where water and possibly a waste tank may go. On top of these there are more psychological considerations. It is likely that you will want to have the main living area near the front, so that passengers can appreciate the view when you're moving, and different people will have different opinions on the ideal proximity between the sleeping area and the bathroom. Whilst on the subject of bathrooms and toilets, most will also prefer to keep these away from the galley area.

When considering your ideal layout also think about traffic. Do you want your bedroom to be part of a main thoroughfare? It may be a good idea to avoid any sharp corners for those moments when you have to rush through the boat from one end to the other. If your previous experience of a boat has been a holiday hire, do not assume that what works for a week or two will work as well all year round – it won't. Your tolerance levels will change and there will be things you do and items you need if you are living aboard that you will actively avoid when you are on holiday, such as a decent set of tools.

Holiday and liveaboard craft will share the same separate living zones, even if the priority attached to each of them may vary. These are:

❖ Galley and Dining Area

❖ Sleeping Area

❖ Bathroom

❖ Living Area

Each of these is considered in turn below, along with some thoughts on an office area and general thoughts on storage, furnishings, lighting and ventilation. This chapter then ends by exploring the merits and challenges of fitting out a boat, along with some outline costs.

Galley and Dining Area

A well-planned galley should be easy to prepare food in, with everything you need to hand. It is not a good idea to have to stand in a walkway when using the sink or the stove, and for this reason an L-shaped galley is a popular idea. In a well-designed galley there should be adequate room for a cooker, oven, grill, fridge, sink/drainer and food storage – experienced liveaboards know to have store cupboard ingredients they can always rustle up a meal with, and even back up staples such as dried milk and tins.

Somewhere, a decision needs to be made on which domestic appliances are really necessary, taking into account the demands placed on electricity elsewhere. Boiled water and toast will tend to be delivered via the hob, whilst appliances such as microwaves and dishwashers begin to fall into the realms of luxury items, the latter not least because of the demands it will also place upon your limited water supply. On the same subject, views on washing machines vary. They tend to be impracticable on smaller boats and will be water and electricity hungry whatever the size of your boat, but these may be compromises worth making (after all, you can make the call on whether or not to use it depending upon water levels and whether you are motoring and therefore generating electricity) if you don't relish washing your clothes in the sink.

If you feel the need to cook on a maritime Aga, weight considerations will demand that this goes near the centre of the boat, thereby dictating many of your layout decisions. Cookers can be stand-alone or built-in, and like most domestic versions, can include an eye-level grill or have the oven and hob as separate. Assuming that you are not always going to be close to an electricity hook-up, fridges and freezers really need to be as close to the batteries as possible, which in turn tends to lead to the galley area being towards the rear of the boat, nearer to the engine. Freezers are useful if you are living aboard, but do consume a lot of electricity and gas, although there are some newer models, which are more economical.

Where the galley is sited will most likely determine the position of the eating area. Whilst this may be a separate area it is more likely that it will be incorporated into the main living area, with this space serving a dual purpose. Equally, as already mentioned, you are unlikely to want to locate your toilets near the galley and already it can be seen how one decision tends to inform the next when it comes to layout design. The reality is that some form of open-plan layout will tend to be the result, with clever design ideas, such as storage areas or bookshelves acting as internal walls, used to break up areas. Not only is open-plan more efficient, but it also makes your interior less claustrophobic.

On the subject of storage, it is vital to have somewhere to store your food, which combines accessibility with tidiness. This is another area where caravan design has had an influence on boats, and their innovative and effective ideas, such as shelves that pull out vertically rather than horizontally to save space. Storage needs to be clever, with no space left unused. Check out how corners are used in any design and look out for good ways to hang items you will need regularly, but not in a way that will allow them to fall should you have a slight altercation with the side of a lock wall or another boat! Kitchen units can be of standard domestic design, with much the same opportunities to add features through design and tiling that you would have in a house.

Bathroom

Bathrooms represent a good example of the different standards that may be applied to a holiday and a liveaboard boat. They are also an area where fittings need to be slightly different from the standard domestic issue. Some kind of shower or sit-in bath is likely to be desirable, as is somewhere to wash clothes, or at least to dry them on those wet autumn days when you can't let them dry in the breeze (although a bath

A sit-in bath can also double up as somewhere to do your washing.

Bunks can be either fold-out or (as shown here) permanent.

does offer the potential to act both as somewhere to wash clothes and somewhere convenient to hang them while they dry). Small baths are by no means out of the question, but your options here are determined by the size of your water tank and water heating capacity.

Vanity units on a boat tend to be built to take into account the limited space, whilst Chapter 5 provides more details on toilet options. The waste tank also needs to be as close to the centre of the boat as possible, otherwise the boat will list noticeably to one side as it fills, offering a rather obvious advertisement as to the state of your tank for anyone observant enough to notice!

As a liveaboard you will also want to think through your fresh water capacity if you are not to be constantly refilling your tank. Equally, if your water is going to stay around longer you may wish to consider a separate supply for drinking water or, as a minimum, some kind of filter. Grey water from the bath or shower usually has to be pumped out of the boat as it is below the waterline.

Sleeping Area

Sleeping accommodation is a further area where attitudes will change if you are spending more than a week or two on board. You will almost certainly prefer a permanent bed to one that you have to assemble every night and scrabble around to find the bedclothes for. Sleeping bags are okay but they are not a long-term solution.

If you are going to live aboard a narrowboat a permanent bed will have to run fore-and-aft, especially if you happen to be over 5ft 10in tall! Other types of bed, for example fold-out bunks (especially good for small children), and tables that convert into a bed using Desmo legs, should not be ruled out – but reserved for guests! The boatman's cabin is a favourite area for guest accommodation. When planning your boat layout also check that the bed is actually long enough, as it has not been unknown for boats to be sold because the 6ft owner made the mistake of buying a boat with a 5ft 6in bed.

The sleeping area is one that offers plenty of potential for ingenuity, especially for storage. The space under the bed is one such area, although this can be used for the water or toilet pump-out tank (even if you wouldn't want to be reminded too often if it was the latter!). Storage above the bed is also a possibility, although care needs to be taken that this does not become a magnet for the top of your head every morning. Whether this is practical will depend on other factors, such as the shape of the walls (most of them slope) and whether or not there is a window – most people like to have a window in the sleeping area.

A bed does need to have air circulating under it if the mattress is not to become mouldy, as many caravan owners will testify. There also needs to be ventilation in the sleeping area – it is surprising how much moisture two adults release into the atmosphere over the course of a night. Finally, a built-in bedside light or ceiling spotlight with a separate switch would be normal in this area.

Living Area

Somewhere to relax and maybe entertain in is an essential component of the liveaboard life. This is your retreat and it needs to be a pleasant, comfortable and above all practical space. It is here that you will locate most of your creature comforts such as entertainment systems, books and whatever – quite literally – floats your boat pastime-wise. The space left over when you've fitted everything else in should not be an afterthought certainly if you wish to avoid cabin fever and claustrophobia. It also shouldn't be untidy or cluttered as this can contribute not only to accidents (that book or piece of equipment carelessly stowed) but also to considerable frustration when you need to find something in a hurry.

Like a living room in a house, the configuration of this retreat may well be driven by whether or not you have a TV, although in a boat it is likely that this will be considerably more modest than many of the monsters now found in many people's homes, not only because of size, but also electricity consumption. At least one comfortable chair is desirable if you have the space, and if you are clever this may be convertible into a guest bed as well.

As already mentioned, the living area may also double up as the eating area and if so a collapsible table, usually hinged from the side of the boat, may be a good idea to create a change in feel. Entertainment systems such as the TV and music are normally housed in a built-in cupboard for their security and protection during the day, and they can later 'come out to play' in the evening.

If you have opted to have a stove (see Chapter 5) then this too will most likely be in the living area, and towards the front of the boat so that smoke from the chimney does not blow into the helmsman's eyes. Living areas also tend to be towards the front of the boat for the reasons touched upon above and because they are then further away from the engine and therefore quieter when you have to recharge the batteries.

A pull-out can convert a single bed to a double.

Built-in units allow for neat and safe storage.

Should this be the case, it is also likely to be near the steps leading up to the foredeck, the space behind which offers a convenient place to locate outdoor shoes.

The living area is also where you are probably going to have your shelving for books, DVDs and so on, and all those knick-knacks that make a boat a home. The shelves will have to have a lip or bar on them to stop items tumbling out at the earliest opportunity, and there is plenty of scope for inventiveness for where you locate them. Have a look at what other people have done before committing yourself – an excellent rule to apply throughout this chapter, with the two main boat shows held at Crick, Northamptonshire, in late May and the IWA's annual event held at various locations over August Bank Holiday weekend both good places to start.

Office Space

Mention has already been made of the possibility of an office space on board a boat. In reality, with laptops it is less the computer itself that takes up the space than all the other paper-based paraphernalia that goes with a modern office, ranging from filing to a printer (top-feed printers have a smaller footprint but for some reason are becoming increasingly hard to find).

The reality, though, is that for better or worse, most lifestyles have begun to incorporate the use of a computer and, love or loathe them, they do offer an excellent way to keep in touch with people when deprived of landline phones. That said, gaining the functionality most homeowners now take for granted isn't easy, with broadband access speeds very much the exception rather than the rule.

If accessing the internet is your main concern, the advent of smartphones and tablets such as the iPad have made life a whole lot easier, although for the most part these still require a decent phone signal to access the web through 3G or 4G. Apps providing GPS and locator services can also be very useful. Equally, Internet access 'dongles' (available from all network suppliers) make access via a laptop much simpler than it used to be, again with the proviso that you can get a mobile signal. If you have to have broadband speeds a satellite link is an increasingly popular option if you also want to guarantee good TV coverage.

The reality is that most liveaboards who need to access the internet at broadband speeds do it using Wi-Fi hotspots, with many marinas, pubs and even coffee shops beginning to cotton onto the commercial potential of offering this, or if needs be by paying for a connection at a local library or cybercafé, which can cost as little as £1–£2 per hour.

Other communications pose similar problems. While it is possible to have a landline telephone if you are permanently moored, the only realistic option if you are on the move is a mobile phone. This is a considerable improvement on only a few years ago when keeping in touch meant studying OS maps for the public telephone symbol. Mobile reception inside a boat (especially if it is metal) tends to be unreliable, though, which can be inconvenient if the weather's bad as you have no other choice than to go outside, and one option here is to fit an external aerial. Unsurprisingly, reception will also disappear when you enter a tunnel, which is just when you might need it most. In response to a tragedy in the Harecastle Tunnel in 2014, mobile coverage was extended to the tunnel in 2016, although at the time of writing the CRT had no plans to extend this to other tunnels.

It's a similar story when it comes to television and if you can't live without the goggle-box then you will need an external aerial or dish (the same is true for radios), although some boaters opt for having a TV and DVD/video and eschew live TV. Once again, it depends on preferred lifestyle.

Storage

Storage has been mentioned more than once in this chapter and its importance cannot be underestimated. The watchword here is ingenuity. Wherever there is a gap consider whether it could be used to store something, especially if it is a hidden gap – but within reason, as you are also trying to avoid a cluttered look.

A good example of this is the engine compartment, which can be used for storing tools, as can other underfloor storage, such as might be available under the foredeck, depending on the location of your water tank. Under-gunwale storage is also often utilised. Clips can also be used to great effect to secure items to walls and ceilings and if you have the space available, think what you might be able to achieve by raising your bed by a foot or so (although remember the need to keep an airflow going).

Cupboard space is another area, with very few liveaboards really needing a full-length cupboard, with a rail halfway down being far more useful. On this subject, also be sure to use the space around your

boiler as an airing cupboard or even drying space, or alternatively use the engine room for the latter if you have an internal engine. Under-seat storage is a must and cupboard space needs to have adjustable shelves to fully utilise the space on offer.

Think of storage in terms of what you want to store. Clothes storage will require different standards than coal for example, and you will want to keep clean and dirty clothes separate. Small items may need stackable containers and most DIY shops offer a range of ingenious storage solutions, as do some of the plastics specialists such as Lakeland and Bettaware.

Finally, think about outside. If you are living aboard, some lockable pods on the roof work well – just look on them as you would the boot of your car. If you have a permanent base, lockable cabinets or even self-storage units are well worth investigating, with most marinas offering facilities of some kind.

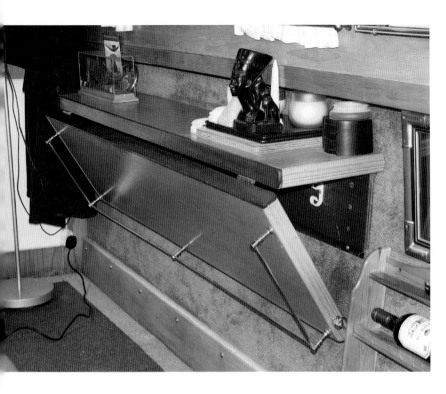

A classic foldaway table.

Furnishings

Both soft and hard furnishings take on different qualities when placed in the context of a boat. Both need to be easily cleaned and compact. Curtains will necessarily be small and constrained by bars to keep them from flapping about, but they offer a rare opportunity to add a dash of colour which will help define the tone of your interior, while at the same time offering a chance to demarcate different areas.

Chairs and other fixed or semi-fixed items of furniture need to be viewed through different eyes. Is there any possibility that they can be turned to more than one use? Can that stool also act as the rest for a fold-out bed, for example, and can that banquette also act as a storage area? The possibilities are endless – you just have to be minded to look for them.

Light and Ventilation

Most boats come fitted with aluminium single-glazed windows as standard, although it is possible to go for higher specifications, including double glazing or anodised windows. The latter are worth considering as it is on the frame that most condensation will gather, and double glazing is also worth investigating, since windows are the most vulnerable point on a boat for thieves and vandals, to say nothing of the insulation benefits, although this does come at a fairly hefty premium for narrowboats and river cruisers.

Portholes tend to be thicker and can feel more romantic, but they do have the downside of letting in less light. This can be a serious issue for the solitary liveaboard, at best inconvenient, and in severe cases even leading to cases of seasonal affective disorder. Alternatively, roof lights may seem like a good option, but they can be prone to leaking. If you really want to incorporate portholes in your home, one idea is to design your boat to have a 'safe area', which uses portholes for its light and is capable of being secured. This can then be used to store your most valuable items when you are away.

Standard domestic double glazing units should be seen as entry-level for houseboats, which, being static, can be more flexible about where they locate their windows. As the houseboat liveaboard knows what their view is going to be, they can decide what it is they want to look out on and what it is they want to avoid!

By their very nature boats tend to be dark environments. For those lucky enough to have access to mains electricity, your lighting options are very similar to a domestic house. Lighting can be a drain on your batteries, especially as you are most likely to be using them when the engine isn't running, and this will necessarily limit the number of lights you can have blazing away at any one time. It may be sensible in some areas to have push-lens battery lights.

A wide variety of styles of light are available, ranging from reproduction Victorian brass through to ultra-modern spotlights in chrome and gold finishes. Once again, think about what your lifestyle is likely to be – will you be doing a lot of reading, for example, and do you want spotlights or something a little more intimate in the sleeping area? Ceiling lights tend to be recessed, for obvious reasons, and whilst wall-mounted lights may look nice they can also be a nuisance if they are on a main thoroughfare. Candles are not advisable, although oil lights remain quite popular for mood lighting, usually gimballed and wall-mounted. They can, however, be dirty and smelly, and should really only be used for effect.

On a similar theme, ventilation is an easily missed consideration on a boat. Liveaboards are essentially living in an enclosed metal, wooden or fibreglass box through all seasons, and efficient ventilation is a must not only to keep a flow of air going but also to provide a means for unwanted gases to escape. Both high- and low-level ventilation are the subject of set marine standards, which have to be followed when fitting out a boat. The most common form of basic ventilation is mushroom vents in the roof, either in traditional brass or stainless steel, although ventilation grilles will also be necessary near any gas appliances. Equally, ventilation is needed to avoid a build up of condensation caused through the simple act of breathing.

To DIY or Not

Once you have decided your basic layout, the question arises whether to do it yourself or get someone else to do it – or maybe a mix of the two. It is possible to buy basic hulls to work on and equally possible to buy an existing boat and convert it to meet your specification – although inevitably this latter option will require some deconstruction before you get into the reconstruction!

This decision may be driven by considerations of time, cost, will and, most important of all, competency. However tempting the option of doing it yourself may seem, if you are to live on board your boat you will be confronted with any errors on a daily basis. Charged with optimism, most potential liveaboards with a hankering to fit out their own boat tend to underestimate each of these considerations and the following is intended to offer some guidelines to help you make some realistic decisions.

When calculating the time required to fit out a boat a rough rule of thumb for the novice is to allow two days per foot of boat, so a 60ft boat would require 120 days. That may not seem too bad but each of these days represents at least eight solid hours at the coalface and excludes any time spent in preparation, planning and shopping. In other words, this assumes you have the materials you need delivered and on hand along with the tools and knowledge to convert them into the finished article. This extra time should not be underestimated.

When it comes to the necessary skills, remember that you will need to be a jack-of-all-trades – carpenter, mechanic, electrician, decorator, gas installer, fitter and plumber. Gas installers must be Gas Safe registered with a LPG certificate. It is unlikely that you will possess all these skills, and some tasks will require a qualified professional to achieve the appropriate certification if nothing else; and getting someone in to do selected tasks will reduce the number of days you will need to spend on those tasks and it should be possible to arrange these to dovetail with your own time, thereby improving the efficiency of the process. It will, however, have an impact on cost.

When it comes to costs these will be driven largely by the level of specification you require and as with all large DIY projects it is prudent to allow a decent contingency on top of any final figure. Budgeting is important and needs to be kept on top of if you are not to end up with a nasty shock. A (very rough) rule of thumb for fitting out costs is anywhere between £150 to £250 per foot.

If you have the time, inclination, skills and finance to do it yourself there's little that can beat the sense of achievement of fitting out your new home yourself. As any regular viewer of Channel 4's *Grand Designs* will know, doing it yourself is always more work than you thought it might be, and usually more expensive too! Equally, as the one example of fitting out a boat used on that show demonstrates, the downside of getting it wrong can be pretty deep!

Questions for Lifestyles and Layouts

- ▶ What is absolutely essential for you to maintain your lifestyle or the lifestyle you aspire to as a liveaboard?

- ▶ What do you want your boat to look like inside, and what feel are you trying to achieve?

- ▶ Are there any fundamental constraints on your layout? Is there anything that has to go in a certain place?

- ▶ How do you want to proportion the interior of the boat? Aim to be open plan to avoid claustrophobia.

- ▶ Will you have enough space to have a permanent bed?

- ▶ Will the layout be suitable for long term living aboard? Don't use holiday boats as a template – look around at what other liveaboards have done.

- ▶ Does your design give you enough ventilation?

- ▶ Will the furniture you buy actually fit through the doorway?

- ▶ Do you have the dual-use storage mindset?

- ▶ Do you want to do the fitting yourself? Consider all the elements involved carefully.

- ▶ Will you be comfortable or cramped? Consider the living area you want. Make sure it isn't simply the space left over after everything else.

CHAPTER 7

ELECTRICS

Electricity is such a fundamental part of modern living that we tend to take it for granted. It is only when we have an unexpected power cut that we realise quite how dependent we are on it. What's more, our reliance on this precious and invisible commodity has increased in recent times, with government statistics showing a rise of 30 per cent per household in domestic use of electricity over the past thirty years.

Whilst there are a number of explanations for this, one important factor is the sheer number of electrical appliances we have and the power required to work them. A good example would be a flat-screen LED TV, which can also double up as a computer screen, and a satellite connection that can also provide digital radio.

These are all luxuries the liveaboard cannot afford, certainly if they intend to cruise. Even if your mooring offers a 240V 'hook up' it can be a salutary experience to watch the numbers showing your consumption click round, and as soon as you slip your mooring you will be on your own, a self-sufficient unit operating under the very simple equation that you will only be able to consume what you can generate, store and transmit.

This chapter will therefore cover these three dimensions of electricity on board and go on to look at what might be considered the fourth leg of the table: consumption. It also includes a brief examination of an often overlooked side effect of electricity when it comes to boating: the damage it can do to your craft and how you can protect it. Before all that, however, it's worth pausing to consider some basics, with apologies to those for whom this is meat and drink.

An onshore electricity hook-up.

Basics

Electricity is a form of power, which is defined as the ability to do work. It is made up of electrons which are too small to see and will flow, if given the chance, around a circuit, and when it does this the flow is known as a current. Although water and electricity are notoriously bad mixers, water can be a useful analogy to use when considering the properties of electricity, which is useful given that water is a major preoccupation of this book! Circuits need to be closed to provide a current and if they are open then the flow automatically stops – in this way electricity is not like water, namely it does not simply flow out of a wire if there is a breach.

The 'strength' of an electrical current is measured in amps, although it is expressed in mathematical terms by the letter 'I'. We will see why this is important in a moment. The driving force behind that flow is known as the voltage or 'V' and the factors within the circuit which impede that flow are known as resistance or 'R', with appliances a good example of resistors, although as we will see there are others.

The relationship between these three components was neatly summed up 180 years ago by Georg Ohm, who devised the simple equation $V=I \times R$, from which it's possible to calculate exactly what's going on within an electrical circuit. Such was the significance of Ohm's discovery that his name is used to describe the SI unit of resistance. Following basic mathematical principles, $V=I \times R$ can also be expressed in other ways such as $R=V/I$ or $I=V/R$. If you know two of the three basic components in your equation (and it is usually easy to get these from labels and packaging) you can use Ohm's Law to calculate the third – for example, if your load has a resistance of 4 ohms and the voltage source is 12V then your current will be 12/4 i.e. 3 amps. Power, expressed as watts, is equally easy to understand using the equation $P=V \times I$, and using these mathematical tools it is easy to grasp what is happening where within your electrical system.

Given your likely reliance on electricity as a liveaboard, this basic understanding will be important to help you regulate your system and make sure it is in balance, as well as to diagnose the inevitable problems when they occur. Not for the liveaboard the luxury of simply assuming the electricity will just happen; you will need to keep a constant eye on the inputs and outputs involved and on maintaining that balance.

Generation

Most electricity on boats is generated as 12V direct current, although it can also be supplied as a 240V alternating current. It is known as alternating current because it is produced using magnets rotating between coils wound in opposite directions, which means that the current produced changes polarity as it is produced, causing the electricity to oscillate in a sine wave, with one complete wave known as a cycle, with the number of cycles a second known as frequency, measured in hertz.

If you have the benefit of mains electricity you will receive AC, whereas if you are generating your own electricity on board and storing it in batteries this will be DC. This is important, as it will determine the sort of circuit you will have on board and how you power appliances – a 240V AC television will not work directly off 12V DC for example. As most liveaboards will want to have the convenience of using 'normal' domestic AC appliances, the solution is to have a means of converting self-generated 12V DC power into 240V AC, which is achieved using an inverter. 12V DC appliances are available, from kettles to TVs, with many produced to be run off car batteries, but they are rarely as satisfactory as the range of ordinary appliances available in every high street shop, and they also tend to be expensive.

Inverters convert 12V DC produced on board into 240V AC, with modern versions also charging your batteries and allowing for a convenient switch between landlines and batteries. They can also act as an energy management system with dials and measures to monitor inputs and outputs, as well as ensuring that you are delivered perfect sine wave power, which is very important if you plan to use a computer on board.

This is where the equations mentioned above become important as when choosing your inverter you will need to have a good idea of what your likely power requirements are going to be – and then add at least 50 per cent if your budget will allow. In practice you will have five main options for sourcing electricity, with the opportunity to 'mix and match' along the way:

❖   A mains electricity link

❖   Engine-driven alternator

❖   Generator

❖   Solar power

❖   Wind power

Mains is the most convenient source, but do not make the mistake of assuming that all you have to do is hook up and you can have as many appliances as you want. In practice, power will be limited and relatively expensive.

An engine-driven alternator is the most common way of generating electricity when on the move. In short your diesel engine is powerful enough to generate DC electricity, which can then be stored in your batteries (see below). This can in turn be passed through the inverter to produce 240V AC. Typically, boats have one battery dedicated to powering the starter motor – so that you won't be left stranded by watching too much TV – and then at least one more to power the domestic system. An alternator will be fitted to charge the former, and on more modern engines another, larger alternator is attached to charge the latter via an extra pulley on the crankshaft.

Separate generators can also be used to produce electricity, using either petrol or diesel. These can be hooked up to provide power straight into your system, although care should be taken to ensure that all 240V circuits are protected by circuit breakers as, being surrounded by water, your system cannot be earthed in the way that a normal domestic system might be. This is not an area for cutting corners. Generators can be relatively compact, measuring as little as a small suitcase, and can be useful for topping up your power if you haven't been cruising and are not near a hook-up.

Generators do offer some disadvantages. Because of the fuel they use and the fumes these give out they have to be kept outside, as do your stocks of fuel, with all the associated security concerns – generators are designed to be portable and as such are tempting targets for thieves. It is possible, however, to buy water-cooled generators that fit into the engine compartment and draw their fuel direct from your main diesel tank. But whichever type you use, they can be noisy and should be used with consideration, especially when near other boaters or in a built-up area. The noise a generator makes can be surprising, even if you are inside watching TV or listening to your favourite rock band on your (electricity-powered) music system.

Solar power is becoming an increasingly popular option as the technology improves, offering both financial and environmental benefits. Generating solar power does require an upfront investment, although costs seem to have levelled out in recent years. The panels often need to be quite large to generate any sensible amount of electricity, and they are unlikely to reliably fulfil all your power requirements. That said, they can be a useful component of your power generation mix.

Solar panels typically use silicon cells and can come in a variety of forms. At one end of the spectrum they may be rigid and framed and may need permanent fixing, while at the other end they can come in flexible 'mats' which can be rolled out along your roof when required and taken in again afterwards. If you opt for permanent panels be aware that this will limit the use of your roof for other purposes, such as storage, flowerpots or even sunbathing.

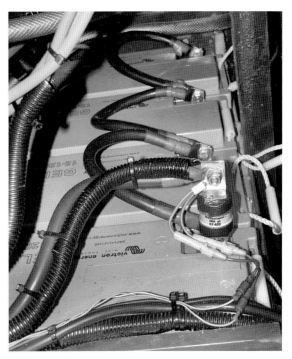

Batteries are often grouped together into banks.

Keeping a generator on board means you are not reliant on the engine for power.

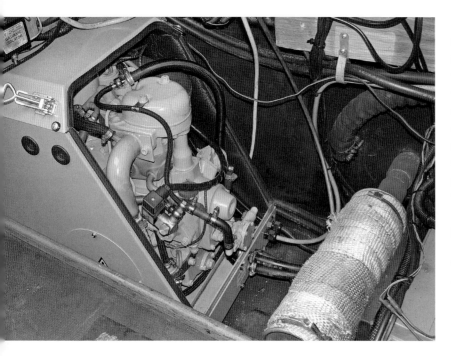

A fitted generator can alleviate security concerns.

One increasingly popular option is to go for adhesive-backed panels, which can be stuck to a roof to fit its curvature, and this is important as one of the determinants of the effectiveness of solar panels is the angle they present to the sun. Access to the sun is another important factor, and the most obvious, as although direct sunlight is not needed to generate electricity it does have a bearing on how much is produced. If you spend a lot of time in the same location you may therefore wish to consider shadows, and more importantly shade from nearby trees, and how these vary across the day and year. Taking these into account can halve the stated power rating of a bank of solar panels – this rating indicates what the panel is capable of, not what it will necessarily deliver.

Once again, solar panels represent an exercise in achieving the best balance – here between surface area, power requirements and cost. In practical terms most panels used on boats can supply around 70W. What does this mean in real terms? Some simple calculations based on the demands of some key appliances can help, such as:

4 x 20W lights used for four hours	= 320W
1 x 40W TV used for three hours	= 120W
1 x 50W water pump used for half an hour	= 25W
TOTAL	= 445W

A 70W solar panel receiving twelve hours of sunlight would in theory generate a total of 840W, but operating on half efficiency would provide only 420W – in other words, a useful contribution but not a total solution, given its unreliability and the fact that this calculation excludes a fridge, the most power-hungry of all appliances, seeing that it is typically on all the time.

Returning to the issue of cost, estimates vary but depending on use, and assuming you live on board all year round, solar panels can have a payback time of between three and five years, although this does not factor in the non-quantifiable benefit of generating your own carbon-free – and noise-free – energy. Panels can be fitted relatively easily but they must have a blocking diode fitted to prevent reverse current flow at night.

Wind power is also attractive from a green perspective and there is a range of small turbines available for the boat owner. Many of the calculations regarding solar power apply equally here, although turbines have their own pros and cons. They can be particularly effective if you tend to stay for long periods in non-sheltered spots (although this may carry other disadvantages), although they need to be erected and taken down each time they are used. The balance here is between size and power, the larger turbines generating more power, but needing more wind to get going in the first place. They can also be quite noisy, unlike solar panels. On the other hand, wind tends to be more plentiful in the non-summer months and a combination of solar and wind energy could provide a useful year-round supplement to your engine-produced power.

Storage

Since you will not be using your power as it's being generated, you need to store it until required. This is achieved using lead-acid batteries, which are essentially a mix of chemicals and metal used to preserve and discharge those little electrons. The secret to good electrical storage lies in battery maintenance, with digital voltmeters a must to monitor condition and capacity. Batteries are also expensive to replace and can represent a significant ongoing cost – they should not be taken for granted. Furthermore, most boats will have more than one battery, with one usually dedicated to starting the boat and others supplying other circuits. It is worth knowing which battery is linked to which circuit; it can help considerably when diagnosing any problems with electrics. Batteries only store what you generate by turning the engine over, they are not an infinite source, and if you are stationary for a long period you will need to top them up.

Batteries should be of the deep cycle or traction type and need to be kept in a well-ventilated compartment as they give off hydrogen gas, which is explosive. Fluid levels should be topped up regularly with distilled water, unless they are of the gel or the maintenance-free, sealed types. As a rule of thumb, aim to cover the lead plates by around ¼in if using distilled water. Although technically 12V, a healthy fully charged battery should be around 13.2V, although anything above 12.5V is okay.

Battery terminals are of critical importance and should be covered to prevent anything metal, such as a dropped spanner, falling across them, which can cause an explosion. Batteries also need to be kept free of corrosion and grease, as this can cause a circuit to form and accelerate the speed at which the batteries discharge. Left on their own, batteries will discharge their power and this can be another benefit of solar panels, which can be wired up to trickle-charge batteries if you have to leave them for periods of time. Smaller 20W units are useful for this purpose. Assuming you have a bank of batteries, these will be wired together and it is worth doing this neatly in order to keep everything obvious, and as part of good 'shipshape' practice.

Transmission

Having generated and stored your electricity, you need to get it to your appliances and make it work for you. This is where your knowledge of Ohm's Law comes to the fore, as moving electricity around means wires, and wires constitute part of the 'R' in $V=IxR$. The longer the wire between an appliance and the batteries the more electricity will be used up getting it there, resulting in a drop in voltage. For this reason, it is better if heavy users of electricity, such as your fridge, are as close to the batteries as possible.

Furthermore, there are clear limits on the thickness of wire required to convey electricity. Too thin and they will get hot and become a potential fire hazard, as well as creating an unnecessary drop in voltage across the length of the boat. Also, Ohm's Law tells us that the lower the voltage the higher the current, which means that a 12V system will require thicker wiring than 240V. All wiring also needs to be protected by the correct fuses. Most liveaboard boats tend to have 240V systems wired as a ring main, with conventional 13A sockets – which also need to be fused.

Consumption

The other side of the generation equation is consumption and there are a number of tricks to use to keep the equation in balance. The first, as hinted at earlier in this book, is to take a serious look at what you actually need, not just in terms of 'stuff', but also in what the 'stuff' consumes. Start by drawing up a list of the absolute necessities and then broaden this out to include 'love to haves' and then a greyer list of 'nice to haves'. Apply your knowledge of the basics of electricity to identify your power needs and start to do deals with yourself over where your priorities lie, and whether you prefer to simplify both your electrical needs and the chore of supporting them, or whether you would rather keep both the gadgets and the difficulty of powering them.

Absolute necessities are likely to include lighting and power for things like pumps. Then consider which form of energy you want to power other necessities such as cooking, heating and the fridge, all of which have gas alternatives. Electricity drawn off your sockets may be used to power gadgets, notably kitchen gadgets such as kettles and possibly toasters (but again, a gas cooker provides a good alternative for both) and

All metal-hulled boats need to be fitted with a sacrificial anode, which needs periodic replacement.

LED light bulbs are now widely available and use much less electricity.

Converting a fluorescent light bulb to LED.

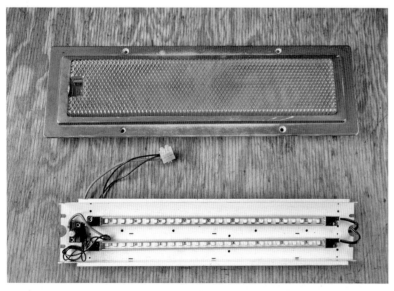

entertainment such as music, TVs, satellite, DVDs and so on. Even within these components there are options, however, such as digital music players and more efficient fridges. The introduction and widespread availability of LED light bulbs has had a significant impact on reducing power usage in boats in recent years and it is possible to convert traditional fluorescent fittings to LED. Electrical luxuries may include dishwashers, washing machines, irons and freezers, and although all these are possible, having them will involve a trade-off against other appliances or additional sources of power.

Protection

Something a boat owner has to consider with regard to mains electricity, especially if they spend a lot of time in a marina or near other boats, is hull corrosion. What is known as a galvanic reaction takes place whereby one boat acts as an anode and an adjacent boat as a cathode, the pair effectively forming a battery with a chemical reaction taking place between them which results in any steel exposed to the water being attacked. This is not something to be taken lightly, with bad pitting sometimes visible on the hulls of two- or three-year-old boats, and some canals and rivers worse than others. The problem will be particularly noticeable where there are two different types of metal involved, with the metal more susceptible to corrosion taking the brunt. This may affect not just hulls but also other metal components in the water, such as propeller shafts.

Steel-hulled boats should, as a matter of course, be fitted with sacrificial anodes, which will corrode before the hull and therefore require regular inspection and replacement as necessary. If they do not rot this could well be a sign that your hull is taking the bulk of the damage. One anode on the bow and one of either side of the stern, with additional anodes along the sides if necessary depending on the length of your boat and local conditions, would be typical, with different types required for salt and fresh water (it is worth checking you get fitted with the right type). Also, the anodes should not be painted over when the hull is blacked and they do need to be kept weed-free, so they are worth checking from time to time.

But anodes on their own may not be enough. Marinas offering mains power tend to do so via cables which are strung together around the earth cable in the shore power leads, and whilst essential for safety these also create an excellent conductor, making it easier for a current to build up and accelerating any potential damage (see diagram top right). The solution to this problem is a galvanic isolator (see diagram bottom right).

In summary then, electricity is something the liveaboard cannot take for granted, with a happy harmony requiring thought and planning. This is true both in terms of balancing generation and consumption, and in creating the most appropriate 'mix' of power sources for your boat, position and lifestyle.

Diagrams courtesy of Safeshore Marine.

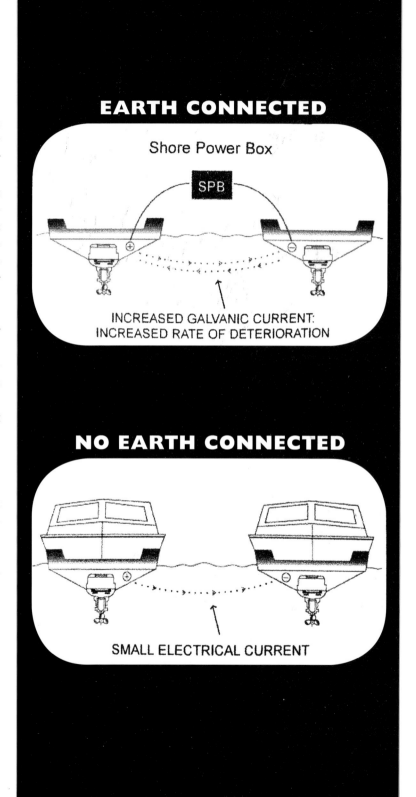

EARTH CONNECTED

Shore Power Box

SPB

INCREASED GALVANIC CURRENT: INCREASED RATE OF DETERIORATION

NO EARTH CONNECTED

SMALL ELECTRICAL CURRENT

Questions for Electrics

▶ What range of appliances do you need to live successfully on board?

▶ What other appliances would you like?

▶ What potential is there in your list of appliances for energy-saving options?

▶ Have you calculated your power requirements? Add some room for manoeuvre and work backwards from this.

▶ Will you be using mains power at any point during the year?

▶ What would you need for your power supply? Balance your power requirements with the different options open to you for generation – remember to include considerations such as convenience, environmental impact, noise and cost in your calculation.

▶ Is the electrical system safe? Have your electrical system checked for long-term reliability and safety. Electricity is one of the few areas with the potential for catastrophe and isn't worth gambling with.

▶ What about corrosion? Make sure your boat is protected against potentially harmful corrosion from below the waterline.

CHAPTER 8

ENGINES

Whether you intend to cruise or not, the one thing you cannot do without as a liveaboard is an engine. Your engine is more than a simple means of propulsion. Unless you have a permanent mooring with mains power or a generator, your engine will be your main source of energy, and as such, lies at the heart of your life-support system. It's surprising, therefore, how often engines are taken for granted, especially when looking round a potential liveaboard craft, when it's all too easy to get caught up in other things such as living space and decoration.

There are a number of things to take into consideration when it comes to engines including their size and type, location, the space they take up, their efficiency and their noise. At its most basic level decisions about your engine will probably involve some level of compromise between image and practicality. You may come to curse that brass-piped beauty you saw on display in the marina when you have to live with it.

Let's start with the most practical consideration for a liveaboard: space. Certain boat styles will dictate where the engine is located. A cruiser-style narrowboat, for example, will have its engine under the deck, out of the living area and still nicely convenient to service and repair – so long as it isn't cold and wet outside. A 'trad' narrowboat, on the other hand, requires the engine to be in what would otherwise be living space. Some vintage-style engines may need as much as a 2m-long separate engine room inside the boat, a sizeable proportion of the total available, and although it may be possible to use some of this space as a utility or drying area, remember that the space will invariably be dirty and smell of diesel.

This is when it is important to remember the dual uses of the engine, since even when you are not moving an engine would typically have to run for two to three hours a day to top up the cabin batteries and heat up water if you don't have a separate boiler. An inboard engine will generate not only power but also a lot of vibration and noise during this time, to say nothing of the fumes. For these reasons excellent ventilation

Gardner engines are renowned for their reliability.

Listers are also a popular choice.

and probably soundproofing are also essential for the liveaboard to consider.

Another important consideration when running an engine is your neighbours, be they fellow boaters or people living in nearby houses. Many areas have local by-laws restricting the running of engines to certain times of day, and signs requesting considerate use are becoming more familiar. Whether or not you run your engine in or out of gear is a matter of personal preference. Some schools of thought suggest an engine will run cooler when in gear and under a working load, but remember that the wash may affect boats moored in the immediate vicinity and local wildlife, and perhaps most important of all, tends to erode the bank. Finally, running an engine in gear is also considerably noisier.

Before considering the relative merits of different types of engine it is worth bearing in mind their origins. Most marine engines are in fact adaptations of automotive or industrial engines; very few are designed specifically for marine use. This is significant because an automotive or industrial engine is built to do a very different job from a marine engine, with an emphasis on delivering power at higher revolutions per minute through the use of gearboxes. A boat, on the other hand, needs an engine that will provide strong, low-speed power at the propeller, which means that a marinised engine needs detuning and low gearing to convert high-speed power into low-speed torque. Add to this the need to protect the engine from water and to configure it in such a way that it is easily accessible (since, for obvious reasons, it is usually not possible to get underneath a marine engine) and one can see why marinised conventional engines usually represent a compromise. The one big advantage of using marinised car or industrial engines, however, is that they do benefit from a worldwide distribution network for spares.

Marine engines offer compromises in other areas also. The fact that they are required to push their burden through water rather than through air adds complications to the balance between power and performance. At the optimum power for a certain hull shape, adding more power will not produce more performance, since increasing power will also increase the hydraulic forces acting against the boat, and hence slow it down. At optimum power the boat is supported by a wave crest at the bow and another at the stern. Add more power and the aft crest moves down to the stern, which has the effect of making the boat want to move uphill.

When it comes to canal boats there are basically two families of engine to choose between. The first is the vintage type, typically slow-revving and delivering high torque, which means these need a large propeller and, in turn, a deeper draft boat. This may be an issue if you intend to live mainly on canals. They are also usually cooled by raw water, which does mean that you have to keep the mud box clean to prevent overheating.

The advantage of this type of engine is their looks, and a well-maintained vintage engine can be a thing of beauty to those of a certain disposition. They also typically have a distinctive sound all of their own, a sort of deep-toned chug which summons up memories of fairgrounds. Traditional names such as Lister, Petter, Gardner, Enfield and Russell Newbury dominate this sector, and having a certain type of engine can be a good icebreaker when meeting new people on the canals.

The other main family of engine is the modern type, usually based on Japanese industrial designs. These would typically be the type of engine offered to a potential liveaboard buying a new boat. Higher-revving, these require a smaller propeller, are quieter, smoother-running and can power three alternators to charge an engine battery, a 12V supply for the marine systems, and a 240V domestic system (see previous chapter for more on electrics). Names here include companies such as Barras Shire, Beta and Vetus. There are also still a number of BMC and Ford-based engines in use. These engines tend to be keel-cooled with a tank built into the swim so that transferring heat into the canal or river cools the engine.

When it comes to what size and make of engine to choose it's best to listen to advice. If you are having a new boat built for you, your boatyard will have its own opinions on which is best, notably in terms of reliability, as they will not want you coming back all the time with problems while it is still under warranty. When listening to recommendations on size it is always worth asking what it would cost to have the next size up – you may find it is only a marginal cost for a benefit you will appreciate for years.

Inevitably perhaps, choosing your engine involves yet a further compromise – here between image and practicality. Either type will do the job but if your main concern is practicality, the more modern engines are probably the best bet. Being higher-revving means that the alternator doesn't have to be geared up so much and some have a cooling system fitted with more than one thermostat that means that the contents of the water tank heats up more quickly via a califorier heating coil.

Most boat engines are fitted towards the bottom of the hull (although not always) and towards the stern. The gearbox allows a simple selection choice of forward, neutral and reverse, whilst also reducing the revolutions of the propeller shaft by around a factor of two in order to improve efficiency. If the engine is fitted on a flexible mounting, which is done to reduce vibration, then the propeller shaft will be connected via a

A Shire engine installation.

A boxed-in super-silent engine.

flexible coupling. The shaft then passes through the hull to the propeller via a stern gland.

A key consideration with engines is their cooling. The sheer amount of work an engine is required to do means that an engine will overheat if there is no system for cooling it. This is achieved either through an air- or water-cooling system. Air-cooling systems are very straightforward, involving a duct and a fan, and so long as both remain in working order the engine should remain cool – although some excess heat should still be expected to emanate from the engine (in fact, most cooling systems only remove about a third of the heat generated). Although cheap and simple, air-cooling systems do have the disadvantage of being noisy.

Simple water-cooled systems use the principle of drawing in water, channelling it through the cylinder block and head, round the exhaust manifold and then back into the river or canal. Whilst much quieter than an air-cooled system, this approach has its own disadvantages. Water drawn into the system inevitably includes impurities and these can accumulate in the pipes. The solution is to use thermostat-controlled heat-exchanging technology, in which fresh water is passed through the engine, and the pipes of hot fresh water are then cooled by contact with cold canal water. It seems a shame to lose all the heat generated by the engine, and many liveaboards consider fitting a calorifier, which looks and acts a bit like an immersion tank in a house system, which can be used to heat water for domestic use. A final consideration here is hoses, as water-cooled systems will involve rubber hoses and these do perish over time, and as such it's always worth having some spare lengths in different sizes.

It is worth pausing to consider the work that you expect an engine to do for you. Anyone who's ever tried to turn an engine manually to see how much power they can generate will soon realise the value of an efficient machine, and also, critically, of a good alternator – the device, which converts the mechanical energy created by the engine into electrical energy. Alternators take a lot of power out of an engine, so it's worth considering just how many electrical devices you want to run off it, as highlighted earlier. This use of the engine is a good reason why few liveaboards choose a river cruiser as their home, as these tend to be powered by outboard engines and need a separate generator to do all the work that an inboard engine would also do for you on a narrowboat.

Access to the engine has already been touched upon and is a key factor. Engines need to be easy to reach, as there are few things worse than having to take your furniture apart every time you want to carry out some basic maintenance, and such work is part of the regular routine of any liveaboard (see Chapter 9). The engine and the gearbox both need to be within easy reach, as running repairs such as changing the fuel filters and adjusting or replacing the alternator belts are both regular jobs.

All the above engines are diesel-fuelled and there are a number of good reasons for this. Not only is petrol dangerous to store and handle, it also tends to need an electrical ignition system and these often find it hard to cope with exposure to damp conditions. It is also more expensive, even after the planned rises in the cost of red diesel (and even its possible abolition) are taken into account. Petrol does have a place in powering marine engines, however, this tends to be confined to outboard motors for smaller, lighter craft. Most boaters are stuck with the smellier and noisier alternative.

There are other types of engine but these are of curiosity value only to the liveaboard, with examples including electric, steam and semi-diesel engines. Electric engines have the advantage of being cheap and easy to operate, although they are practical only for very light boats. Other options of more interest include hydraulic drives, which offer more freedom on the critical question of where to locate the engine and can be worth considering.

Whilst considering the engine compartment, it's here that you will find the weed hatch, a way of accessing the propeller without having to pull on the waders. This comes into its own when your propeller snags on debris in the water, often something plastic such as a discarded agricultural bag, an eventuality that is sadly inevitable at some point. At its worst, when this happens you know in no uncertain terms through the complaining noise emanating from the engine, a juddering, or a sudden loss of power. The procedure when this happens is to moor, turn your engine off completely and begin the process of feeling your way around the propeller to see what the problem is – albeit gingerly at first as the offending material might be sharp. If necessary, use a Stanley knife or even an old kitchen knife to loosen things up a bit. As has probably become clear here, caution is the watchword. When finished, wash your hands thoroughly.

A final and often overlooked feature of marine engines is the stern gland. This acts as the interface between the prop shaft and the propeller, and as such is where the water meets your engine compartment. Usually full of packing material, most stern glands have graphite impregnated square profile rope that is wound around the prop shaft and then tightened down into a compression gate. This is then 'fed' grease, via a tube, with a plunger or tap providing the necessary pressure. Giving a couple of turns on the tap is a regular job, especially when on the move, and from time to time the reservoir containing the grease needs to be topped up. By definition, this can be a messy job, although one tends to get better at it over time.

Questions for Engines

▶ Inside or outside – where would you prefer the engine to be?

▶ Old or new? Do you want a thing of beauty, which will need more maintenance (and might this even be a pleasure for you?) or do you want something more practical?

▶ Decided on new? If you are buying new consider going to the next size up, as it may only be a marginal extra cost for a significant benefit over time.

▶ Which cooling system – air or water?

▶ What about the engine? Make sure you can get at your engine to conduct regular maintenance.

CHAPTER 9

FINANCE

Having got this far into this book, and assuming your appetite to live aboard has been whetted, you've probably been on a journey that has oscillated between desire and trepidation but is now nearing its end with one great question still hanging in the air: how much is all this going to cost me? The answer, as is so often the case when it comes to money, is that it depends.

That said, this chapter will set out some rough rules of thumb and an indication of what you might be letting yourself in for. Before getting down to brass tacks, it is worth emphasising the truism that with boating, as with so many other things, you get what you pay for. When budgeting to live aboard, there are plenty of opportunities to prioritise expenditure according to your own personal preferences and chosen lifestyle.

As a general rule, it's probably fair to say that living on board your own boat is much less expensive than living on shore, but don't make the mistake of thinking that the costs are insignificant – they're not. Those who ignore some of the basic maintenance costs outlined here will find that 'economies' are nothing of the kind and will come back to bite you very quickly, and that they have the capacity to bite quite hard! It is also worth keeping in mind that whilst house prices tend to go up much faster than inflation, at least in the medium term, an investment in a boat is much less likely to produce a significant dividend over time.

Given the wide range of variables, and bearing in mind that the inland waterways remain the choice of the vast majority of liveaboards, the numbers discussed below are based upon a mid-sized (55ft) narrowboat, although they should provide a good template for others as well. An assumption has also been made that you already own your own boat, and no allowance has been made for financing the cost of buying in the first place. While on the subject, you can expect to pay anything between £25,000 to three times that for a decent mid-sized second-hand liveaboard narrowboat of this size, a price that rises for a wide beam or other specialist craft, or indeed for a new narrowboat, and is of course dependent on age and condition. The final section of this chapter considers some of the detail of buying your own boat.

Fixed Costs

There are certain costs you simply won't be able to avoid, but some latitude remains on how high you let them climb. No allowance has been made for depreciation, although if you follow the guidelines set out below, you should find that your boat holds its value fairly well. Your absolute fixed costs will be your licence and insurance, although as will become apparent, this isn't the end of the story.

Licence

Licence fees will vary according to where you want to cruise. If you intend to take full advantage of the inland waterways system, taking in both the rivers controlled by the Environment Agency and the canals operated by the CRT, you will need a Gold Licence. The cost of the licence varies according to the size and type of the boat, but as a general guideline, a licence for our benchmark 55ft narrowboat in 2016–17 was £1,356 if paid by direct debit, £100 less for prompt payment, more for staged payments. If you are happy with staying on the canals and rivers administered by the CRT, you can limit yourself to their licence (and buy a short term licence for the EA's waterways as required), which costs £933 for our benchmark boat (£840 for prompt payment). In addition, there are discounts if you can demonstrate your boat is historical or powered only by electricity.

If you have a houseboat with no means of propulsion at all, you need to apply for a Houseboat Certificate, although this costs the same as a Canals and Rivers Licence. A houseboat is defined as 'a boat whose predominant use is for a purpose other than navigation' and has to have planning permission, if required, for the site where it is moored. If you

Houseboats without a means of propulsion need a Houseboat Certificate, but this costs the same as a CRT licence.

intend to trade from your boat, you will need a Business Licence, with a Roving Traders and Fixed Trading Licence costing around £1,000 for a 55ft boat. If you own a boat but want to let it as a residential boat, then you will need a Residential Lettings Licence, costing £1,772 for the same boat, still with the 10 per cent discount for prompt payment.

It is difficult to overemphasise the importance of getting the right licence and making sure you keep on top of renewals. Whether they like it or not, the liveaboard is essentially 'camping out' on waterways that are the responsibility of the relevant authorities. They are not, as some might assume, some kind of national resource free for all, like common land. Authorities such as the CRT retain quite draconian powers to enforce their will, and instances of boats being physically lifted out of canals for non-payment of licence fees are not unknown.

Insurance

It is a requirement of your licence that you hold, as a minimum, £2 million of third-party insurance. The key words here are 'as a minimum' as it is likely, especially as your boat will also be your home, that you will want to go for a comprehensive policy, especially given the marginal cost difference involved and the fact that your boat will very possibly be your biggest asset. The waterways press includes a number of advertisements from marine brokers and the market is fairly competitive.

All in all, for our sample boat expect to pay around £350 a year in total for insurance (including contents). If your boat is also your prime residence you will also need to take into account your possessions and the need to cover them. Insuring anything is rarely straightforward these days, with the devil sitting well hidden in the detail. As such, liveaboards need to take special care when selecting the most appropriate policy, making sure they are not just covering the hull or other basics, and being realistic as to the value of your possessions. Insurers have got better at recognising the liveaboard community, but the onus is on the person taking out the insurance to inform the insurers of their status when taking out the insurance, something easily forgotten by those who segue from pleasure boating into living permanently on their craft. It is worth shopping around between insurers, but be aware that some will take the opportunity to demand a fresh survey when taking you on, even if you are able to produce one only a year or two old. This is especially the case with older boats, with an age of twenty years a common threshold to automatically trigger a fresh survey.

Those trading from their boat need to
apply for a Business Licence.

HULL BLACKING
UP TO 62FT

£10 FT + VAT

BOOK NOW FOR AUTUMN
WINTER

01225 722292

←

END OF SOMERSET COAL CANAL

• OTHER DRY DOCK
  SERVICES AVAILABLE

• GAS
• PUMPOUT CARDS

Hull blacking is a regular expense that
shouldn't be skimped on.

Council Tax

If you decide to live on a permanent houseboat, another fixed cost
will be council tax, which will of course vary enormously according to
where you choose to live but a (very) rough rule of thumb suggests
you shouldn't expect to pay less than £1,000 per annum. If you are
renting your houseboat and your finances are constrained, you may be
entitled to apply for housing benefit, which can help with the costs of
the rent for the boat, mooring fees and the licence. Continuous cruisers
and most other boats with at least the ability to move should find that
they can avoid council tax, although, again, local authorities vary in their
interpretation of the rules.

Maintenance

Although there is only one absolute fixed cost under this heading – the
requirement to renew your Boat Safety Certificate – this brings with it
other costs too. The cost of the survey required to gain the certificate is
fairly modest, especially when factored in over four years – you should
allow around £250 for the survey and the inevitable niggles that will need
to be resolved, probably because the regulations have changed since you
last had it done – but the process itself acts as a good discipline to get
other sizeable but necessary jobs done at the same time.

The most obvious of these is getting the hull blacked. Views vary on
how frequently you should have your hull blacked but the four-yearly
cycle of the BSS operates as a powerful incentive to get your boat lifted
completely out of the water (the cost of this has been included in the
amount quoted above) and have a decent look around. Fresh anodes will
also be necessary at this point. All told, a reasonable sum to set aside for
this would be £500, although it is probably fair to say that four years is
the absolute maximum you should leave blacking and every two years
is better for budgeting – so, that's £250 a year, which makes an annual
allowance of £300 plus when BSS and associated work is annualised
and added.

Likewise, it's difficult to determine a precise interval for repainting, as
your need will depend upon how many minor scrapes you have, the basic
condition of your superstructure, the quality of the previous paint job,
how decorative and intricate you want to be and whether you've gone

off your existing colour scheme. Painting is also something that many liveaboards like to get involved with themselves, viewing touching up paintwork as an ongoing and not altogether unpleasant task.

Nothing quite beats taking your superstructure right back to bare metal and applying even coats of the various primers and undercoats required to provide the 100 per cent protection from the elements that you will need. Let's say you decide to have a back to metal job done once every five years and keep on top of things yourself in the meantime. A professional stem-to-stern job, stripping back to metal and applying the various coats will cost in the region of £100 a foot, so that's £5,500 for our 55ft boat, or £1,100 a year. On top of this you need to add materials for regular maintenance and you will be looking at a minimum of £1,200 a year – a significant cost that is often underestimated.

It is possible to reduce this sum considerably, probably to a quarter of this, if you do it yourself and don't factor in your labour costs (a good job may take three weeks of your time, although this is assuming constant fine weather, a possibly rash assumption in the UK, even in summer). Costs are not just the paint itself, which is intrinsically expensive in the first place, but also equipment, consumables and, ideally, a painting tent. DIY paint jobs are usually easily spotted – the boats never quite look as if they are finished – and unless you have been on a course, a specialist signwriter should be employed for the name, with a guideline of £30 a letter.

Finally, assuming you are not a master mechanic, an annual service is probably a good idea. Again, this is not an absolute necessity but gambling on nothing going wrong is a high-risk strategy – you really don't want to get stranded in the middle of nowhere and have to find someone who'll come out to see you: a call-out charge will soon make you rue not having that regular check-up. At a minimum, your filters and belts should be checked and probably replaced, and it's a good idea to have the electrics and gas looked over as a matter of course. Once again, therefore, this has been included as a fixed cost and a fairly reasonable one at that – say £200. Add a little more if you want to buy the extra peace of mind of knowing you will be able to call out a professional at will, something you can secure by joining one of the various canal and river rescue companies which act as a sorting of boater's AA – details are available in the waterways press.

A run of liveaboards.

Variable Costs

Variable costs cover those items where you might think you have greater latitude, and whilst this is true to some extent, it is surprising how quickly those bills accumulate no matter how hard you might try to keep them down. The main variable costs are moorings and consumables, although once again, there are many others.

Moorings

The subject of moorings has been given its own chapter in this book and this serves to demonstrate the range of options – and costs – involved. The absolute minimum you can pay is nothing, assuming you either adhere to the continuous cruising rules, even in winter, or have some kind of arrangement with a kindly landowner. Both of these are likely to be the exception. The next step up is probably the boater who cruises for most of the year but moors up on a CRT site for, say, four months a year, which may cost as little as £500.

More likely scenarios involve a part-time base, although again, costs will vary according to whether this is on the towpath or in a marina, and those with a long-term base. As with most things in life you will get what you pay for. A marina mooring for example will include some services and it depends on where in the country you want to be, as mooring prices tend to echo house prices in this regard. Equally, as already highlighted, not all marinas are open to long-term residents.

For this reason, no single figure has been given for moorings, as it could only represent an average and would therefore either be misleading or meaningless. If you want to go towards the bottom end of the scale, budget at around £750 per year, and if you want to head towards the more comprehensive end, allow around £4,000 per year. These figures are for the canals, and rivers will be significantly more, as will urban moorings. Also, if your home is a houseboat you probably want to move out of a mooring cost mindset and think more in terms of rent.

Consumables

Basic consumables will include gas and electricity (whether metered or generated yourself), fuel, and pump-outs. Gas will be bottled and you will need to keep a spare bottle at all times. Assuming you don't use gas for heating, a budget of around £250 per year might cover your needs, though double this if you do use it for heating – the difference being a

reasonable budget for coal and wood (although it is possible for forage for the latter). A bag of coal costs around £12 and a typical liveaboard will consume three bags a week during a cold spell. Metered electricity has the advantage of allowing you to monitor use and security of supply, but this comes at a cost – in the region of £125 assuming you are only using it in the winter and are cruising the rest of the year.

Fuel will depend upon how much you cruise and run your engine, and this is where the hidden cost of generating your own electricity resides. Recent rule changes now require the purchasers of red diesel to declare an expected split of use for cruising and power generation, with different VAT rates applicable to each. This confused, and confusing system, is something of a nightmare, although some retailers of diesel will offer some guidelines so a reasonable rate can be calculated. Alternatively, continuous cruisers in particular are advised to keep a record of the hours they spend cruising, so a spilt can be calculated, and this isn't a bad idea for all. As a very rough rule of thumb, running an engine costs around £1 an hour, a figure that certainly focuses the mind when you are recharging your batteries. On this subject, it's worth having a voltmeter to let you know when you have got to full power to avoid unnecessary expense. All in all, we estimate an annual budget of £500 for diesel seems reasonable for higher-end mileage.

Pump-outs are a necessary cost, assuming you have this kind of arrangement, and is a cost that can accumulate. It can cost as much as £250 per year, depending upon how many are on your boat and assuming you don't have your own kit, but even where this is the case there will be a disposal charge and you may wish to consider whether the effort required to make the saving is worth it.

Other costs are mostly discretionary, although it is advisable to factor in the cost of some running repairs and routine maintenance, as well as a sum to treat yourself to a fresh piece of kit, or to replace consumables such as batteries – which only last three to four years – into your annual budget. Say £500 for that. Items falling into the discretionary area have cropped up during the course of this book and include things such as onshore storage, a car parking space, a post office box and costs associated with mobile communications. Few liveaboards will be able to avoid all of these, and as such a contingency sum of £500 has been included here to be spent as you choose, which may be a little on the conservative side.

Summary

Rough Annual Liveaboard Budget

Licence	£840–£1,200
Insurance	£350–£500
BSS and annual maintenance	£300–£500
Painting	£500–£1,200
Annual service	£200
Cooking and heating	£250–£500
Diesel	£300
Pump-outs	£250
Other repairs, maintenance and equipment	£500
Sundry other costs	£500

Taking all these costs together suggests a sum in the range of between £4,000–£6,000 a year for our nominal boat, although this excludes moorings, which could easily be half as much again, any metered electricity and any council tax. These figures should only be regarded as very rough guidelines and will vary according to your situation and relative priorities. They will also vary depending upon how many people are living on the boat. Given the high level of unavoidable costs, expenditure per head will fall considerably if there is more than one person resident on the boat.

Buying A Boat

Before you get involved with annual running costs you will, of course, have to buy your boat in the first place – assuming that owning your own boat is your goal, as is the case with the vast majority of liveaboards. While many boat purchases do not require financing as they are funded from proceeds elsewhere (the sale of a house, a legacy, a retirement or redundancy package), many others do, and it is worth pausing to consider some of the rules of this particular game.

Few conventional financial institutions regard buying a boat in the same way as buying a house. In recent times even housing has lost its allure as an asset against which banks and building societies are willing to loan money, so their attitude towards giving credit for a boat can be imagined. These institutions are likely to require something more tangible before they lend on a boat, and if you intend to retain a pied-à-terre for the winter months, one option may to be raise a mortgage on this. Otherwise, banks and building societies will probably only lend you the money on an unsecured basis, with all the implications this brings for interest rates.

Luckily, marine finance specialists exist, and it's worth looking online and in the waterways press to see who is active in this area at any one time. Again, it is worth checking the waterways press for lenders who understand the idiosyncrasies of the boating world, but even these institutions are unlikely to offer you 100 per cent loans, with 70–80 per cent closer to the norm. Some loans are regarded as marine mortgages – that is, although the rate charged is lower than with a normal loan, the sum is secured against the boat – whilst others may be unsecured. As with houses, a survey and independent valuation will also be required. If the craft you intend to live on is one capable of traversing the high seas, you will find your creditworthiness sinking faster than an anchor, as lenders have a (perhaps understandable) fear that you may never be seen again!

This is only a brief introduction, and isn't designed to frighten potential purchasers, just to inject some reality. If you look like a reasonable risk and have a good credit history, you can expect to be offered a plethora of products – secured and unsecured, fixed and variable rates, mortgages and loans and even personalised packages. As such, independent advice may be a good idea, and there are plenty of brokers available to help you negotiate a way through the maze (again, see the waterways press), and going down the broker route may even end up saving you money in the long run.

Questions for **Finance**

▶ Have you got the right type of licence?

▶ Have you checked whether you will need to pay council tax?

▶ Have you included a budget for recurring maintenance?

▶ How much of your own painting do you intend to do?

▶ What about your mooring options? They may represent as much as half your annual running costs so need consideration.

▶ Will you be paying for metered electricity?

▶ Decided on buying a boat? Use a marine finance specialist and consider using a broker.

CHAPTER 10

GENERAL MAINTENANCE

As may have become apparent by now, living on board a boat requires a fair bit of dedication and knowledge, although, as with anything, this becomes less daunting the more it becomes part of your routine. It's all about adopting a fresh mindset. As part of this, there are a number of what might be called general maintenance tasks you will need to keep on top of, some of which have been alluded to already.

The aim of this chapter, therefore, is to highlight the most critical of these, and to help you understand what to look out for and how to approach the issues that arise. As a liveaboard, being able to tackle many of the tasks set out in this chapter will become essential life skills, and even if you do not do them all yourself, you will need to know what it is that needs doing and to be able to check that they have been done correctly.

The Hull

Your boat's hull is like the roof on your house, the main difference being that you can't put a bucket under it when it springs a leak. Your boat hull can be thought of as a tank, with any water or dampness accumulating in the lowest part of the bilges. Not only does water enter the hull from any leak, however small, below the waterline, but also from leaking hatch covers in the roof, leaking window frames (a very common problem), and any other container containing liquid on your boat, notably your water and pump-out tanks.

Leaks are always a problem, the trick being to trace them back to the source and tackle them there – rather than simply where they manifest. Hatch covers can be especially tricky as you may be dealing with anything from a faulty seal to a design fault in the boat, whereas window leaks are easier to tackle. If the leak is only a small one, some silicon sealant will probably do the job. If it is more serious, caused by a build-up of rust between the cabin sides and the frame, then the frame itself will have to be removed, the rust treated and the frame primed and resealed with an all-weather sealant.

Always be on the lookout for dry rot, especially under any carpet.

Leaking plumbing or a damaged tank are clearly more major tasks for which you may need expert help. Your responsibility is to be on the lookout for potential leaks, and to do this it is a good idea to have a piece of flooring that can be easily removed to access the bilges at the lowest point in the boat, which effectively acts as a sump. This should be inspected every month. Any build-up of water should be treated as a warning sign, and should be mopped or sucked out using a wet vac. At the same time it is a good idea to have some ventilation under the floor to prevent dry rot starting in the floor or bearers. If you have the luxury of building your boat from new, it may be worth considering protecting the bilges with a coat of Waxoyl before ballasting.

Perhaps the most common problem encountered with plumbing is pipes that burst during winter due to frost, which only become apparent when the water is turned back on when returning to the boat and the pump keeps going. Because of this, the cautious liveaboard will always turn the water pump off when leaving their boat.

Shot-blasting in action.

Keeping on top of paintwork on the superstructure is a good idea.

The subject of hull blacking has been touched on elsewhere in this book, and this should be seen as a regular act of maintenance which should be budgeted for. This applies to steel-hulled boats, which need to be lifted completely out of the water (beware of so-called dry docks which do not run completely dry) so that their hulls can be cleaned off and repainted. Ideally this should involve cleaning all the weed and rust off the hull using a grit-blaster, which is a specialist job and can be quite expensive.

The alternative to grit-blasting is to use a power washer, and if you go down this route it should be done as soon as the boat is out of the water and the hull is still wet. Older craft may need regular professional inspections to satisfy your insurance company and if this is the case, this is the ideal opportunity to have a survey carried out by a marine surveyor.

When the hull has dried off, all loose rust needs to be removed using a wire brush and the surface needs to be treated with an antirust preparation such as Rylard Rust Konverta. If you choose to use a bitumen-based paint (hull black), the manufacturer will recommend it should be applied to bare steel, so do not prime with red oxide or zinc primer. Bitugard is made from coal tar and pitch, and Comastic has vinyl added to the tar and pitch.

Hull black is a very thick paint so it needs to be applied using a large brush and rubber gloves. Eye protection must be worn at all times, and one-piece overalls and a hat are also recommended. More than one coat should be applied and you will need to follow the instructions on the tin, with some manufacturers recommending four coats on bare steel. The paint must be left to dry for at least twenty-four hours before returning the boat to the water. Two pack epoxy coatings are becoming more popular and, although initially more expensive, the paint will offer better protection and is more hard-wearing so it may be worthwhile. A further option that has recently become available is Zinga, which is a one-component anti-corrosion zinc coating that provides environmentally safe cathodic protection to steel and can be applied as though it were a paint. If you are using a third party for your hull blacking, an unannounced check to see that they are doing things correctly can be a good idea, as once the boat is back in the water you have no way of checking. Some boatyards will try to get away with a single coat, but this isn't enough.

Similarly, seagoing craft or those moored in tidal waters need to be coated with an anti-fouling paint once the weeds and barnacles have been removed. An anti-fouling paint suitable for freshwater inland waterways has also recently become available from Rylard.

A selection from the range of available hull coatings.

Using a water lance to clean off a hull.

The Cabin and Superstructure

The more visible part of your boat above the waterline also needs regular attention and the first step is to make sure you keep the paintwork in good condition by washing off the algae, moss, bird droppings and leaves, making sure that you clear drainage holes as you go along. Like car washing, this can be a relaxing Sunday afternoon activity, although you need to be careful when washing the non-towpath side of your boat, when a long-handled brush can come in handy if you don't feel like turning the boat around.

Car shampoo or wash 'n' wax type preparations are fine, but ensure that whatever you use is friendly to the environment as it will be going straight into the water. Any sign of rust or chipped paint needs attending to sooner rather than later, as once rust gets under the paintwork it will spread very quickly. The rust will need grinding out, treating and priming before touching up with matching paint.

The superstructure of a narrowboat may need repainting once every four to five years, and this can be an expensive job so it's worth planning ahead and doing some research into preferred paints and colours. Some colours are more durable than others, with red particularly vulnerable to fading. For all but the very skilled, painting is a professional job and once again it is worth overseeing the work to make sure it is done correctly. In particular, you should check that the correct number of coats is applied – a call to the paint manufacturer will reveal the recommended coverage. Similarly, good signwriting can define the quality of a new paint job, so ask to see examples of the signwriter's work beforehand as these will usually be specialists drafted in specifically for the task.

Water Tanks

Fresh water tanks can be made of polypropylene, stainless steel or mild steel and are integral to the hull. A tank can hold 150 gallons of fresh water and, as these tanks are usually located below the waterline, a pressurising pump is needed to make it flow to the domestic system. If the tank is made from stainless steel, polypropylene or galvanised steel it should be maintenance free, provided that once a year sterilising tablets are dissolved in a full tank of water, as per the instructions on the packet.

Should the tank be integral to the hull under the forward cockpit deck, as is popular on narrowboats, it will be fitted with an inspection hatch. This needs removing once every two or three years to inspect, clean and paint inside the tank as the interior will become full of plant life and rust and quite put you off making a cup of tea from it.

There is only one way to clean this out – get inside and scrub! This isn't a pleasant or easy job but it is very important and should not be neglected. A 'wet vac' vacuum cleaner is indispensable, both for this job and for cleaning out the bilges, but is something that can be borrowed or hired. Having cleaned the tank out, let it dry thoroughly, and then give it at least two coats of bitumen paint. Some hull blacks are suitable for this, but you should check the manufacturer's recommendations on the tin first. The inspection hatch needs to be replaced with a new gasket or silicon sealer, and it is a good idea to use stainless steel or brass bolts to secure the hatch cover so they can be easily removed next time.

Engine Servicing

It is worthwhile getting to know your engine and what, quite literally, makes it tick. Regular maintenance will not only give you peace of mind but also reduce the chances of an emergency call-out, which can be an expensive and time-consuming business. Any diesel engine needs regular oil changes, as set out in the operating manual. Deciding when to change the oil and filter will depend on how many hours the engine has been run since the last service, and you may wish to consider installing an hour counter within the revs counter or a separate gauge. Before the old oil is drained out, run the engine until it is at its working temperature.

Use the sump pump – if fitted – to pump the old oil out, otherwise sump drain plug will have to be removed. If there is not room under the engine for a waste oil container, drop it into the bilges under the engine, then suck it out later with a wet vac. After this, remove the old oil filter and fit a new one, fitting new sealing 'O' rings if the filter is not of the spin-off type. Rubber gloves should always be worn when handling old engine oil, as it is carcinogenic. Check the service manual for the correct grade and type of oil with which to refill the sump, as using the wrong oil can invalidate the engine manufacturer's warranty.

The fuel system on a boat is all-important – nine times out of ten any problem encountered with a diesel engine will be due to problems with the fuel system. Owing to the fact that the fuel tank is in a damp environment and subject to internal condensation, it is always best to keep the tank as full as possible – especially during the winter months. Many of the problems encountered with the fuel system are caused by water contamination in the fuel.

At the bottom of the fuel filter there is usually a drain plug. To meet BSS regulations this must be metal and not plastic, so that it can't melt if there is a fire and let the fuel pour out. Undo the screw periodically and drain into a transparent container (ideally glass) until all the water is removed and pure and clean diesel is coming out. The fuel, being lighter, will float on top of any water. Replace the drain plug. Having done this you shouldn't have to bleed the system. Should the engine still fail or misfire, the next thing to replace is the fuel filter.

Fuel filters come in two main types – the older CAV replaceable element or the later screw-on type. Be aware that there may be more than one filter in the fuel line. Start by turning the fuel off at the tank – something you should check how to do from the manufacturer's instructions, as it is inevitable that at some point you will need to know how to do it – and then follow the instructions supplied with the filter. After fitting, turn the fuel tap back on and finish by bleeding the system – again, each engine is different and you will need to refer to the manual.

On the subject of fuel, red diesel users need to use additives such as those available from Soltron or Morris Lubricants (there are others) to stop 'red diesel bug', an algae that can build up if the fuel is left for a few months, which can go on to block fuel filters. Another good preventative is to keep the tank full over winter, as already alluded to.

Other Regular Tasks

Alternator and water pump drive belts need to be checked for cracks or wear and adjusted at least once a year (possibly as part of a pre-winter routine), and replaced as necessary. Another important part of any pre-winter routine is checking your engine's cooling system, notably making sure it is protected with a strong enough antifreeze solution. This can be checked using a hydrometer, an accessory available from most car part shops, and you should be looking for a minimum of 40 per cent antifreeze. Having added antifreeze, the engine should be run up to operating temperature to make sure that it has mixed properly and circulated around the calorifier tanks. This also provides an opportunity to check for any hose leaks. The antifreeze should be left in year-round as it also acts as a rust inhibitor. As raw water-cooled engines do not use antifreeze it is advisable here to drain the system before the first frost.

While in the engine compartment it is also worth checking the stern gear. Grease needs to be sent down to the stern gear every other day when cruising, using the stern tube greaser provided, and from time to

Keeping good and neat ropes is one of the easiest maintenance tasks.

time the grease supply will need replenishing. Should the stern tube gland start leaking, the solution is not, as is often thought, to send more grease down, but to either adjust the lock nuts which will need tightening, or to repack the gland. Automatic bilge pumps will also need to be checked to ensure they are operational and are clean. Failure to do so can be costly, as pumping oil out into the water is not only antisocial but can also result in a heavy fine.

Other pre-winter checks will involve the domestic heating system. Any central heating system will also need filling with antifreeze/rust inhibitor, with a 50 per cent mix advisable here. It is also a good idea to have an annual boiler service using a qualified engineer. Note that 'qualified' here means not just qualified to domestic standards but also having the necessary certification relating to LPG work on boats and caravans.

If you have a diesel stove, just before winter is also a good time to carry out the unpleasant task of having it de-coked and serviced. If you use a real fire then you will also need to clean out the chimney. This is a job best tackled from the top down using a brush and rod. Remove the baffle plate first and let the soot fall into the fire where it is more easily removed – a dirty but necessary job, which needs to be carried out once a month if you are living aboard to avoid the risk of carbon monoxide poisoning.

It can be all too easy to forget the state of your mooring ropes, which should be checked regularly for rot or fraying. Ropes used to moor a boat on a tidal river will necessarily receive more wear than those used on a boat in a non-tidal river or canal, and all ropes are more susceptible to rot in the winter. A snapped rope is every boater's nightmare, especially if it happens at night, and preventing it is perhaps one of the easiest of all the regular maintenance tasks. When checking your ropes, it's worth giving your staging the once-over if you are on a permanent or semi-permanent mooring. Once again, rot and algae are the enemies here and you don't want the staging to give away, as if it does it will inevitably happen when you have your arms full of something precious, besides which a broken leg isn't much fun on a boat!

Finally, make sure you have both a gangplank and pole that are fit for purpose. It's easy to ignore these as you may only need them on an occasional basis, but when you need them, for example if you get stuck on silt, this is not the time to discover that rot has taken hold when you weren't looking.

Be Prepared

Things will go wrong with your boat, so it's best to be prepared for when they do so. Understanding the preventative maintenance basics highlighted in this chapter is half the battle, being able to cope with the unexpected is the other. With boatyards typically charging somewhere between £40 and £60 an hour, often plus a call-out fee, having the ability to distinguish between a major and a minor problem, and knowing how to contain the former and fix the latter may save you a fortune over time. Background reading, or even going on a course to get some 'hands-on' experience, is also typically time well spent.

A decent set of tools and spares is also an essential, and below we have set out a 'Get Out Of Trouble' list, which taken together would probably cost around £100 to acquire, and probably prove to be the best investment any serious liveaboard could make.

Tools

❖ Set of spanners – metric, SAE or BSF/BSW depending on your type of engine plus a large adjustable spanner
❖ Hammer
❖ Pair of pliers
❖ Assorted screwdrivers
❖ Wire cutters
❖ Hacksaw
❖ Woodsaw
❖ Set of Drills
❖ Set of Allen keys
❖ Mole wrench
❖ Centrepunch
❖ Stanley knife
❖ Wirebrush
❖ Wood chisel
❖ File
❖ Funnel
❖ Multimeter
❖ Latex gloves, or pairs of thin plastic gloves for dispensing diesel collected from filling stations

Spares

- ❖ Fuel filter
- ❖ Alternator belts
- ❖ Hose clips
- ❖ Engine oil
- ❖ Antifreeze
- ❖ Sterntube packing
- ❖ Sterntube grease
- ❖ Distilled water
- ❖ Insulating tape
- ❖ Electrical wire
- ❖ Steel wire
- ❖ Assorted nuts and bolts
- ❖ Assorted woodscrews
- ❖ Mixed nails
- ❖ Jointing compound
- ❖ Wood glue
- ❖ Spare fuses
- ❖ Handcleaner
- ❖ Degreaser
- ❖ Spare plastic water pipe fittings

A good set of spanners should form the cornerstone of a decent toolkit.

If you are not mechanically minded, one option is to buy a membership of a marine breakdown assistance organisation, like an AA or RAC for the waterways, the most popular of which is probably River and Canal Rescue (www.rivercanalrescue.co.uk), who offer four tiers of membership, ranging from just over £50 to over £200, depending on the level of cover required.

Questions and notes for General Maintenance

- Check the bilges regularly and regard any build up of water as a warning sign.

- Fix leaks as soon as you spot them, making sure you tackle the source not just the symptom.

- Hull blacking and superstructure painting can be planned for and do not come cheap – make sure you get a quality job.

- A clean water tank is essential for your health – check it regularly.

- Engine servicing, notably oil and fuel filters and the fuel system, is something you can learn to do yourself, but check you have done them correctly.

- Consider drawing up a pre-winter checklist of maintenance tasks, including the engine cooling system and the domestic heating systems.

- Are your bilge pumps efficient?

- Good ropes give peace of mind.

- Do you have a good set of tools and spares?

- Is your staging sound?

CHAPTER II

SURVIVAL TIPS

So far this book has set out a host of advice to those considering the liveaboard life, but there is nothing that quite beats the smack of experience, so in this final chapter the authors have taken the opportunity to share some of their own survival experience, in the hope that elements of it may distil into wisdom.

This is not intended to be a comprehensive list, more a random collection of tips, and much of what is covered here may seem obvious. But we have taken the view that that is no reason not to state it, since after all, one person's obvious may be another person's revelation; and the obvious has a disconcerting habit of being forgotten! We have clustered these tips under three headings: Safety, Security and Sharing.

Safety

The most basic of all safety survival tips is to have a good first-aid kit. This is not the same as buying an off-the-shelf pack from your local chemist, but means thinking about likely contingencies and stocking up accordingly. Most standard first-aid kits are long on bandages and short on medicines and you need to supplement them with a range of the sorts of day-to-day remedies you may need to dip into and may find difficult to get hold of when you are miles away from a doctor, dentist or pharmacy. Examples may include:

Make sure your dream doesn't become a nightmare!

- ❖ Antiseptic creams, including nettle and sting creams
- ❖ Painkillers such as paracetamol or ibuprofen
- ❖ Cold remedies
- ❖ Something to tackle food poisoning
- ❖ Antihistamines
- ❖ Deep pain spray
- ❖ An eyebath
- ❖ A spare pair of spectacles
- ❖ Antacids

Always ensure that lifebelts are to hand (although you may need to store them inside when away from your boat).

It may also be a good idea to top up your first-aid knowledge by going on a course run by a recognised organisation such as St John's Ambulance before embarking upon the liveaboard life, and to stock up on things like insect repellent and disinfectant. Finally on the subject of health, if you are on regular medication it is probably as well to have a spare supply with you.

Other aspects of basic safety should not be taken for granted, including making sure that lifebelts and jackets are in good working order and are to hand. The same applies to fire extinguishers. Also, while on the subject of the basics, it pays to never keep your eye off your stocks of essentials such as food, fuel and water – easily forgotten, but missed when they are not there. With water it is also worth considering the state of your water tank – do you need a filter for drinking water?

Other chapters have mentioned basic equipment you need to keep to hand, but experience also suggests you may wish to consider an alternative to one of your most elemental items of kit – matches, which have a tendency to get damp as soon as you turn your back. Alternatives include cigarette lighters or hand-held sparkers. Domestic batteries can also start to corrode when you least expect it, so a spare dynamo or solar-powered torch can also be a godsend.

Other items the liveaboard should always have spares of include fuel filters, a full set of drive belts and a tube of silicone, along with some plastic padding to effect a temporary repair should you spring a leak. Think also about keeping a strong magnet on the end of a rope for recovering keys (and even windlass handles) that fall into the water. Most marine key rings have a cork ball or other float, but it is worth testing that this is sufficient to keep your set of keys afloat rather than simply assuming it will – although make sure you have a net underneath first or use a bucket for the test. On the subject of recovering items dropped in the canal, a useful tip is to mark exactly where it fell on the bank before fishing around to find it, as the boat may move in the meantime and you lose the exact spot. Finally, just in case your cosy home becomes a tempting option as the nights draw in, a mousetrap or two may come in handy.

Experience also suggests that it's a good idea to know where you are in non-canal terms. So as well as having a canal guide, it's always worth having a road map on board should you need to jump ship and re-engage with the wider world. Being surrounded by water, you may also wish to have a 'Plan B' should your mobile phone end up in the drink. Record all your most important phone numbers in a book which you keep in a safe, dry place, since if you do lose your phone you don't want to lose all your numbers too. Alternatively, invest in a SIM card backup device or make sure you are backed up to a cloud service. On the subject of phone numbers, it's a good idea to keep all relevant CRT and Environment Agency numbers handy in case of a sudden emergency – a laminated card being one option.

Considering where you moor is also another key determinant of your personal safety. Remember that conditions do change from season to season, and what might have seemed a perfect spot in the summer can be hopeless in the winter, especially if you get cut off by ice or snow – canals can freeze over! Equally, river levels can change and climate change seems to be bringing with it more extreme weather patterns, as witnessed by the increasing frequency of bad floods on our waterways. Finally, in the case of utter disaster do bear in mind the vital importance of having more than one means of escape from your boat!

Security

Protecting yourself from the more unsavoury elements of society is as much a fact of life on board a boat as it is living in a house. If anything, boats should be regarded as more vulnerable – not only because they are harder to protect, but also because as strangers to an area, cruising liveaboards may be less aware of the dangers particular areas may bring.

Boats do get broken into, although instances of this are perhaps more unusual than popular myth may have you believe. Most break-ins are opportunistic, and there is much you can do to reduce the opportunities your boat offers to thieves in the first place. Much of this is common sense, such as not advertising that you have something worth stealing by leaving items of value on display near a window, or making sure you leave curtains closed when leaving your boat. Other sensible precautions might be to leave a (battery) radio on, or to put a log in the fire to make sure there's smoke coming out of the chimney. Also consider what might be thought of as an item of value – this isn't necessarily just consumer goods, which may be of interest to a petty thief, but also food and alcohol, which may attract itinerants or teenagers.

The idea of a 'safe area' that can be given reinforced security within your boat has already been suggested in an earlier chapter. Another good idea can be to bolt a safe to the floor under your bed for really important documents and other valuables. Finally, don't forget the items you routinely leave outside the cabin, which may include poles (handy for smashing windows), flowerpots (likewise), windlasses, lifebelts and

It can snow on the canals too!

A cratch cover can shield a thief.

A security bar acts as an effective deterrent.

decorative items. Some boats also have removable seating, which offers another useful implement to the opportunistic thief. Larger items such as bicycles and fishing gear can be padlocked to the handrail of the boat.

Attention paid to making access to your boat more difficult is rarely wasted. Most thieves like to get in and out quickly and will thank you for having a cratch cover over your front cabin doors, as this provides them with cover while they work on your elaborate security measures. On the other hand, they will not thank you for forcing them to squeeze through narrow windows, so this is an area where portholes offer a benefit, and the sight of someone climbing into a boat via the roof usually arouses suspicions – so long as they can be seen. Boaters tend to operate a very effective informal neighbourhood watch system, and will look out for one another's boats.

Good locks and solid doors should go without saying, but there are considerations here. Steel doors secured with an effective mortice lock are preferable to wooden doors secured with a padlock (which acts as a signal that you are out). Window frames should be riveted and not easily unscrewed, and you may wish to consider fitting security grills or bars.

As well as thieves, boaters need to protect themselves against what politicians have come to call 'anti-social behaviour' – what most of us may regard as yobs and vandals. The actions of this crowd are rarely logical and can be extremely irritating, especially when cruising, and all the more so if you are transparently by yourself. Never underestimate the capacity of the individual with nothing better to do or too much drink inside them to simply throw your things into the water, or even cast your boat off, 'for a laugh', although quite who finds their actions amusing is open to question.

As it happens, instances of stone throwing, rope cutting and 'steaming' (i.e. groups jumping onto one end of your boat and running through, picking up what they can and jumping off the other end before you know what's hit you) are actually pretty rare. Your best defence is probably to be on your guard in unsavoury areas and to have a digital camera on hand (although not somewhere where it can be snatched!), or the camera on your phone. It can be a curiously powerful deterrent if a potential miscreant thinks they are going to be identified after the event.

Finally on the subject of security, all instances of theft and vandalism should be reported to the authorities. Whilst the chances of a successful prosecution in individual cases are slim, an accumulation of reports can spur the police into action and help prevent future incidents.

Sharing

There is a tendency to look at the liveaboard life as a solitary activity, and whilst this is often the case, it isn't necessarily so. By definition, narrowboats are the least amenable craft for sharing, although plenty do share with a partner and sometimes even with children. But it is more usual with larger boats, in particular houseboats. Of course, having children on board opens up a fresh set of considerations, including the range of equipment required, different tastes in entertainment, and especially water safety. Then there's access to friends, health services and school to consider. All these issues are solvable, but involve an extra layer of considerations.

Pets can be easier to live with, especially if they live in a cage! Birds, hamsters and even rabbits and guinea pigs have all been known to provide company to liveaboards. Portable hutches and foldable runs are available, with the runs making it possible for your companion to feel the grass beneath their paws when moored at a grassy towpath.

Dogs are of course a boaters' favourite and although preferences over breed vary, expedience means that the smaller varieties are more popular. Unless your chosen breed is a natural swimmer, the ideal situation is to start them young, with dogs taught to swim as a puppy using a harness or buoyancy aids. Dogs also have a tendency to roam, and a collar tag saying where they live with a mobile number on it are a must. Equally, some kind of fencing may be required to make sure they stay on board when you're close to leaving.

Cats' aversion to water is well known, but this doesn't mean they cannot act as a companion on a boat. Training will be required however, and, being intrinsically less obedient than dogs, cats may need to be corralled well in advance of setting off on the next leg of a cruise if you don't want to hang around waiting for them to come home after a towpath foray. The same logic applies during a cruise – you don't want

to draw up at a mooring only to find your cat jumped ship earlier in the day and now could be anywhere within a 10-mile radius. It's also a good idea to check that they haven't chosen the engine compartment as a convenient place for a nap before you set off. Both cats and dogs should be chipped in case all else fails.

Finally, perhaps the greatest survival tip of all is to recognise that however much you might appreciate your own company, becoming a liveaboard brings with it membership of a wider community. How actively you choose to participate in this community is up to you, but those who ignore it altogether tend to end up being the losers.

Being a liveaboard will mean there will be times when you will need to give and receive favours or just need someone else to talk to, and this will mean tapping into the wider network of like-minded souls. The liveaboard community acts as an informal network which includes those close to you, such as your neighbours, as well as more virtual members, such as other liveaboards you may only see occasionally but keep in touch with, possibly via an internet forum or social media. Taken together, this community represents a vast body of knowledge, experience and society you will not want to isolate yourself from, and indeed hopefully will want to contribute to. Successful liveaboards tend to be those who get the personal balance right between enjoying the freedom living on board a boat offers with the benefits of being part of a wider body of people.

LEARNING MORE

Organisations

There's a wealth of information out there available from the various organisations representing different parts of our waterways, with the following amongst the most significant:

Association of Waterways Cruising Clubs
Focuses on emergency help and overnight moorings for members of affiliated clubs.
Website: www.awcc.org.uk

British Marine Federation
Covers the British marine and leisure industry.
Marine House, Thorpe Lea Road,
Egham, Surrey TW20 8BF
Tel: 01784 473377
Website: www.britishmarine.co.uk

Canal and River Trust
Responsible for the canals and some rivers.
First Floor North, Station House,
500 Elder Gate,
Milton Keynes MK9 1BB
Tel: 0303 0404040
Website: www.canalrivertrust.org.uk

Broads Authority
Responsible for the Broads.
Yare House, 62–64 Thorpe Road,
Norwich, Norfolk NR1 1RY
Tel: 01603 610734
Website: www.broads-authority.gov.uk

Dutch Barge Association
For anyone interested in or who owns a barge.
Tel: 07000 227437
Website: www.barges.org

Environment Agency
Responsible for inland rivers.
National Customer Contact Centre,
PO Box 544, Rotherham
S60 1BY
Tel: 03708 506506
Website: www.environment-agency.gov.uk

Inland Waterways Association
Advocate for securing the future of the waterways.
Island House, Moor Road,
Chesham HP5 1WA
Tel: 01494 783453
Website: www.waterways.org.uk

National Association of Boat Owners
Represents private boat owners.
NABO General Secretary, PO Box 104,
Leyland, PR25 9AN
Tel: 07989 441674
Website: www.nabo.org.uk

Residential Boat Owners' Association
Represents liveaboard boaters and also publish useful booklets on living aboard and on council tax.
Website: www.rboa.org.uk

Royal Yachting Association
Represents pleasure boating and also run Inland Helmsman's Certificate scheme.
RYA House, Ensign Way, Hamble,
Southampton, Hampshire
SO31 4YA
Tel: 023 8060 4100
Website: www.rya.org.uk

Scottish Canals
Responsible for the Scottish canal network.
Canal House, Applecross Street,
Glasgow G4 9SP
Tel: 0141 332 6936
Website: www.scottishcanals.co.uk

Waterway Recovery Group
Dedicated to restoring derelict canals.
Island House, Moor Road,
Chesham HP5 1WA
Tel: 01494 783453
Website: www.wrg.org.uk

Websites

The following is a selection of the many waterway-related sites on the web:

www.canaljunction.com/boat/electrics.htm – list of marine electrical and electronic equipment suppliers and engineers
www.canaljunction.com/boat/systems.htm#plum – list of suppliers of boat heating, water, gas and sanitation suppliers and engineers
www.canalrivertrust.org.uk – Canal and River Trust
www.canals.com – comprehensive site on all things to do with canals
www.justcanals.com – claims to list most canal sites
www.leesan.com – for more on toilet options – includes a handy list of pump-out locations
www.livingonboats.co.uk – useful site with some good articles on specific issues

Books

The following is a brief selection of waterways-related books:

General
Brown, Dan M. *The Narrowboat Lad* series (Kindle Direct Publishing)
Condor, Tony *Canal Boats and Barges* (Shire Books, 2004)
Cooper, Bill *Sell Up and Cruise The Inland Waterways* (Adlard Coles, 2010)
Corble, Nick *Britain's Canals: A Handbook* (Amberley Publishing, 2010, Revised 2016)
Corble, Nick *The Narrowboat Story* (The History Press, 2012)
Davenport, Sheila *Canal and River Cruising: The IWA Manual* (Fernhurst Books, 1998)
Jones, Toby *The Liveaboard Guide* (Adlard Coles, 2012)
Paget-Tomlinson, Edward & Lewery, A.J. *Colours of the Cut* (Landscape Press, 2004)

Specifics
Barrell, Emrhys *The Inland Waterways Manual* (Adlard Coles Nautical, 2013)
Billingham, Nick *Narrow Boats Care and Maintenance* (Helmsman Books, 1995)
Booth, Graham & Burnett, Andy *The Narrowboat Builder's Book* (Waterways World, 1999)
Booth, Graham *Narrowboat Planning – Designing the Interior of Your Boat* (Waterways World, 2005)
Brotherton, Miner & Sherman, Ed *The 12 Volt Bible for Boats* (Thomas Reed Publications, 2003)
Burnett, Andrew *The Inland Boat Owner's Book* (Waterways World, 2000)
Cookson, Gary *A Home Afloat – Stories of Living Aboard Vessels of all Shapes and Sizes* (Thomas Reed Publications, 2008)
Manley, Pat *Essential Boat Electrics* (Fernhurst Books, 2014)
Manley, Pat *Simple Boat Maintenance* (Fernhurst Books, 2014)
McGrath, Cavin *Living Off The Grid On A Narrowboat* (Kindle Direct Publishing, 2015)